Simon Geissbühler (Ed.)

Democracy and Democracy Promotion in a Fractured World

Democracy and Democracy Promotion in a Fractured World

Challenges – Resilience – Innovation

edited by

Simon Geissbühler

LIT

This publication was financed by the Peace and Human Rights Division of the Swiss Federal Department of Foreign Affairs.

The contents do not necessarily reflect the views of the Government of Switzerland.

This book is printed on acid-free paper.

Bibliographic information published by the Deutsche Nationalbibliothek
The Deutsche Nationalbibliothek lists this publication in the Deutsche Nationalbibliografie; detailed bibliographic data are available on the Internet at https://dnb.dnb.de.

ISBN 978-3-643-80390-0 (pb)
ISBN 978-3-643-85390-5 (PDF)
ISBN 978-3-643-85392-9 (OA)
DOI: https://doi.org/10.52038/9783643803900

A catalogue record for this book is available from the British Library.

A catalogue record for this book is available from the Library of Congress.

© LIT VERLAG GmbH & Co. KG Wien,
Zweigniederlassung Zürich 2023
Flössergasse 10
CH-8001 Zürich
Tel. +41 (0) 78-307 91 24
E-Mail: zuerich@lit-verlag.ch   https://www.lit-verlag.ch
Distribution:
In North America: Casemate Publishers, e-mail: casemate@casematepublishers.com
In the UK: Global Book Marketing, e-mail: mo@centralbooks.com
In Germany: LIT Verlag Fresnostr. 2, D-48159 Münster
Tel. +49 (0) 2 51-620 32 22, Fax +49 (0) 2 51-922 60 99, e-mail: vertrieb@lit-verlag.de

Table of Contents

Introduction 1
Simon GEISSBÜHLER

Democracy and Democracy Promotion – The Basics

Why and How Should International Cooperation Promote Democracy? An Introduction 15
Erika SCHLÄPPI

Supporting Democracy – Of, By, and For the People. 41
Bruno KAUFMANN

A Revival for International Democracy Support? 67
Richard YOUNGS

A Conflict Resolution Perspective on Democracy Promotion 89
Lukas PROBST LOPEZ

Table of Contents

Current Democratic Challenges and Opportunities

Elections as a Pathway to Democracy – Challenges in Practice for the Diplomatic Community. 107

Hannah ROBERTS

Protecting Democracy in the Digital Age . . 127

Idayat HASSAN

Spheres of Action in a Divided World 141

Bruno MAÇÃES

Democracy Promotion Through Power-Sharing: The Role of Mediators' Constitutional Templates. 159

Daniel BOCHSLER & Andreas JUON

Country Examples

Towards an Action-Oriented Democracy Diplomacy Agenda 187

Simon GEISSBÜHLER

Three Moments in Democracy Promotion
Practices of Costa Rica: Towards an
Aggregative Process? 209
Alonso VILLALOBOS-JIMÉNEZ

Democracy Diplomacy as Integral Part of
Sustainable Development 237
Patricia DANZI

Introduction

Simon GEISSBÜHLER

Democracy – the rule of, by and for the people – is both old and new.[1] As an idea, it has been a focus of interest and debate among philosophers since Greek antiquity. As a real-world institution and form of government and governance, it was successfully – albeit partially – implemented in ancient Athens. The proto-democratic institution of public assemblies, however, predated ancient Greek democracy by around 2,000 years and was relatively widespread in Syria-Mesopotamia and later on the Indian subcontinent.[2] The end of

---

[1] The contributions in this volume represent a wide array of viewpoints. They are a testimony to the diversity of democracy. While the Peace and Human Rights Division of the Swiss Federal Department of Foreign Affairs financed this publication and welcomes the pluralism of ideas that can and should inspire our work, the views and opinions expressed by the authors do not necessarily represent the positions of the Swiss Government. I thank my colleagues Lukas Probst, Rahel Brugger and Kristina Hoffet for comments on an earlier draft of this introduction.

[2] Keane, John (2023). *The Shortest History of Democracy*. Exeter; also see: Schemeil, Yves (2000). Democ-

democratic rule in Athens was not the end of democracy. Public assemblies, for example, were widely used in many parts of the world for centuries – mostly in local, small-scale settings and contexts.

Democracy reappeared on the world stage in earnest with the founding of the United States of America. It then swept over the globe in four waves, beginning with a "slow" and "long" first wave starting in the 1820s, a huge second one after World War Two, a third one in the 1970s and 1980s, and a final wave after 1989/91, at a moment that was wrongfully and naively seen by some as the final victory of liberal democracy.[3] The four waves "have varied widely in their origins, intensity, and success rates",[4] and

---

racy before Democracy?, *International Political Science Review* 22(2): 99-120; Evans, Geoffrey (1958). Ancient Mesopotamian Assemblies, *Journal of the American Oriental Society* 78(1): 1-11.

[3] The model of three waves of democratization was famously coined by the American political scientist Samuel Huntington. In my view, the model still holds. I would, however, introduce a fourth wave – the one starting with the collapse of the Soviet Union and its sphere of influence. The fourth wave is quantitatively and especially qualitatively clearly different from the third. See: Huntington, Samuel P. (1991). Democracy's Third Wave, *Journal of Democracy* 2(2): 12-34.

[4] Gunitsky, Seva (2018). Democratic Waves in Historical Perspective, *Perspectives on Politics* 16(3): 634-651.

Introduction

all of them have been followed by democratic ebbs or backsliding.

For almost twenty years now, democracy has been in retreat worldwide; its erosion "has become globally pervasive".[5] The V-Dem Report 2023 paints a grim picture regarding the state of democracy today: Advances in global levels of democracy made over the last 35 years have been wiped out; 72% of the world's population lived in autocracies by 2022; and the level of democracy enjoyed by the average global citizen in 2022 was down to 1986 levels.[6] Some even believe that we are heading towards an "authoritarian century".[7] States, groups, and individuals actively work on undermining democracy from within and from the outside.[8]

While democracies differ considerably and while there is no clear dividing line between what would still be considered a democracy and what is already an autocracy, democracies

---

[5] Gamboa, Laura (2022). *Resisting Backsliding. Opposition Strategies against the Erosion of Democracy*. Cambridge, p. 237.
[6] Papada, Evie et al. (2023). *Defiance in the Face of Autocratization. Democracy Report 2023.* Gothenburg: Varieties of Democracy Institute.
[7] Ibrahim, Azeem (2022). *Authoritarian Century. Omens of a Post-Liberal Future*. London.
[8] Mandraud, Isabelle/Théron, Julien (2023). *Le Pacte des Autocrates*. Paris.

do share some basic common features and institutions, values and key elements of a democratic political culture. At its core, democracy combines credible elections and possibly other mechanisms of participation with the rule of law, equal fundamental rights and protections, and institutional checks and balances. At the same time, what we mean when we talk about democracy is ever-changing – but it is also fundamentally stable as it is based on a profound understanding of human nature and deeply held universal principles.

What is called democracy promotion, assistance or support has also come under increased pressure in the last two decades and continues to need conceptual revitalization and new ideas. It is constantly adapted due to geopolitical changes, new challenges, and the understanding that democratic reformers need support to solidify their democratic and economic gains quickly to make sure that the populations who upended the old order get some "tangible dividends in their own lives".[9]

In Switzerland and in Swiss foreign policy, there is a renewed interest in democracy and democracy promotion. This interest predates the Rus-

---

[9] Power, Samantha (2023). How Democracy Can Win, *Foreign Affairs* 102(2). 22-37.

sian war against Ukraine, but it was undoubtedly sharpened by what transpired after February 24, 2022. The then-President of the Swiss Confederation, Ignazio Cassis, underlined in a programmatic speech in August 2022 that we live through a *"Zeitenwende"*, in which core interests and values in general and democracy, in particular, are coming under increasing pressure. As for democracy promotion, he stated: "The promotion of democracy is a task given to us by the Federal Constitution. In this regard, Switzerland can and will do more. We can support other states in strengthening their democracies – if they ask us to do so. We will do this without missionary fervor. […] Vis-à-vis non-democratic states, we will self-confidently defend our core values. This is part of our interest-based foreign policy".[10]

Fostering a constructive, inclusive, and self-critical dialogue and knowledge transfer among democracies, especially in the field of democracy promotion, is part of this. There is a need for conceptual clarification since concepts in democracy diplomacy remain spongy and elusive. Against this backdrop, the Peace and Human Rights Division of the Swiss Federal Department of For-

---

[10] Cassis, Ignazio (2022). *Rede – Auslandschweizer-Kongress 2022*: https://www.admin.ch/gov/de/start/dokumentation/medienmitteilungen.msg-id-90005.html.

eign Affairs organized a senior officials' democracy retreat with renowned international experts in early 2022. The main goal of the retreat was to bring a diverse group of countries together and to have a fresh look at their respective and multifaceted experiences in democracy and democracy promotion. A second retreat followed in early 2023. This volume is partly an outcome of these retreats.

The contributors to this volume tackle different key issues when it comes to democracy promotion and discuss the overall framework within which democracy thrives or dies. The volume at hand is diverse in many aspects. First, the contributors represent a variety of actors and observers in the field of democracy and democracy promotion. In the present volume, the reader will find contributions from researchers, intellectuals, experts from the field, public officials and policymakers, thus representing a broad bandwidth of voices and perspectives.

Second, the contributions focus on a wide array of topics. Some authors revisit basic principles of democratic governance in their contributions, but from innovative viewpoints and with open minds to the challenges and opportunities of today. For example, *Bruno Kaufmann* looks at opportunities for increased civic participation from below and outside state platforms, whereas *Hannah Roberts* focuses on challenges for the diplomatic community to support transparent and credible elections in today's digital age. The digital revolution is a recurring topic, and many contributions touch upon its effects on democracy: *Idayat Hassan* explores how technology impacts our information landscape and discusses ways to tackle disinformation to ensure informed decision-making – a prerequisite for democratic governance.

Freedom of expression and other fundamental rights and freedoms are key topics in other articles as well, including *Erika Schläppi*'s contribution. Fundamental rights and freedoms are not only a basis of democratic governance but also one of the reasons why we assume that democracy is desirable. Many contributions discuss the geopolitical context of the ongoing worldwide democratic recession and the erosion of civil and political rights, rule of law, and compromise, as well as their reasons and possible political and policy responses: *Bruno Maçães* discusses possible spheres of action in a divided world with antithetical values, and *Richard Youngs* first analyzes the overall evolution of international democracy support in the last thirty years and then asks how the current democratic momentum can be taken forward. *Lukas Probst Lopez* argues that rooting democracy promotion in conflict resolution provides many practical benefits and that a stronger narrative around the advantages of democratic governance should focus on democracy's potential to prevent, manage and resolve conflict.

Two articles focus on democracy promotion practice and its future in two countries: *Alonso Villalobos-Jiménez* looks at three key moments of Costa Rica's democracy promotion practice and the potential of a more aggregative process in the future, whereas *Simon Geissbühler* discusses how Switzerland could implement an action-oriented democracy diplomacy in the coming years. Other authors focus on specific aspects of democracy promotion: *Patrizia Danzi* looks through a development lens at democracy diplomacy, and *Daniel Bochsler* and *Andreas Juon* analyze how mediators' constitutional templates influence the power-sharing models in emerging democracies.

I agree with Sergei Guriev and Daniel Treisman that today's pessimism about the future of democracy "is a bit overdone" and that we have "a powerful idea" to unite around, "the idea of liberal democracy".[11] This volume's outlook

---

[11] Guriev, Sergei/Treisman, Daniel (2022). *Spin Dictators. The Changing Face of Tyranny in the 21st Century*. Prince-

Introduction

is rather optimistic. Democracy works, also in "hard places". But it works only if and when political actors support it, when solid inclusive institutions protect it, when it yields some tangible economic benefits and when internal and external support is strong.[12]

Democracies function and are resilient. Broadly based and legitimized decisions and the capability to self-correct seem to have undeniable advantages. In the medium and long term, democracies have more stable and sustainable growth rates and economic policies than autocracies. Studies show that there is a significant positive correlation between democracy on the one and freedom, peace, development, and innovation on the other hand. Democracy allows for debate, dissent, and the plurality of voices. The difference in opinions is its starting point and strength.[13]

In many countries around the globe, citizens, especially young people, fight for more freedom and participation and demand accountability from their leaders. We often say that democracy is the worst form of government – except

---

ton/Oxford, p. ix., p. 219.

[12] Mainwaring, Scott/Masoud, Tarek (eds.) (2022). *Democracy in Hard Places*. Oxford.

[13] Gerhardt, Volker (2023). *Individuum und Menschheit. Eine Philosophie der Demokratie*. München, p. 292.

for all the others that have been tried. I humbly disagree. Democracy is much more than that. It is far from perfect. But maybe it is even – at least sometimes – as a French author recently stipulated – a party![14]

Literature

Cassis, Ignazio (2022). *Rede – Auslandschweizer-Kongress 2022*: https://www.admin.ch/gov/de/start/dokumentation/medienmitteilungen.msg-id-90005.html.

Escoubès, Frank (2023). *Pop démocratie. La démocratie est (aussi) une fête*. La Tour-d'Aigues.

Evans, Geoffrey (1958). Ancient Mesopotamian Assemblies, *Journal of the American Oriental Society* 78(1): 1-11.

Gamboa, Laura (2022). *Resisting Backsliding. Opposition Strategies against the Erosion of Democracy*. Cambridge.

Gerhardt, Volker (2023). *Individuum und Menschheit. Eine Philosophie der Demokratie*. München.

Gunitsky, Seva (2018). Democratic Waves in Historical Perspective, *Perspectives on Politics* 16(3): 634-651.

---

[14] Escoubès, Frank (2023). *Pop démocratie. La démocratie est (aussi) une fête*. La Tour-d'Aigues.

Guriev, Sergei/Treisman, Daniel (2022). *Spin Dictators. The Changing Face of Tyranny in the 21st Century*. Princeton/Oxford.

Ibrahim, Azeem (2022). *Authoritarian Century. Omens of a Post-Liberal Future*. London.

Keane, John (2023). *The Shortest History of Democracy*. Exeter.

Mainwaring, Scott/Masoud, Tarek (eds.) (2022). *Democracy in Hard Places*. Oxford.

Mandraud, Isabelle/Théron, Julien (2023). Le Pacte des Autocrates. Paris.

Papada, Evie et al. (2023). *Defiance in the Face of Autocratization. Democracy Report 2023*. Gothenburg (Varieties of Democracy Institute).

Power, Samantha (2023). How Democracy Can Win, *Foreign Affairs* 102(2). 22-37.

Schemeil, Yves (2000). Democracy before Democracy?, *International Political Science Review* 22(2): 99-120.

Democracy and Democracy Promotion – The Basics

Why and How Should International Cooperation Promote Democracy? An Introduction

Erika SCHLÄPPI

What is "democracy", and why are we assuming that democracy is desirable? What can international cooperation do to support – and revive – democracy? Particularly the first question has been addressed in many ways since the "rule of the people" (*demos* and *kratos*) was identified by the old Greeks as a form of government two and a half thousand years ago. This article aims to provide a short introduction and overview of current practical thinking around these issues.

What is Democracy?

There is no common definition of "democracy". Many countries call themselves democratic, yet in practice, there are many forms of democracy: No two systems are identical, and there is no "one-size-fits-all" democracy that could serve as a blueprint for others.

Nevertheless, there are some common features among the different democratic systems. Almost all modern democracies include aspects of representation: In many countries, citizens are not directly involved in lawmaking and governance ("direct democracy") but elect representatives to do so on their behalf. Free, fair, and transparent elections of political powerholders are perceived as a minimal key feature of any representative democracy, ensuring that the "people's" voices are reflected in political decision-making. Different formats of representative democracies can be distinguished: Parliamentarian or presidential, unitarian or federalist, with proportional electoral arrangements or "winner takes all", based on two-party or multi-party systems, majoritarian or consensual approaches. In the view of many, democracy has an important legitimizing function for powerholders; it offers political processes for the peaceful transition of power and helps political systems adapt and respond to new challenges.

However, democracy goes far beyond ensuring a formal electoral process to select representatives and legitimize powerholders. Free and fair election processes responding to quality standards are important conditions but not sufficient for guaranteeing democracy. For example, the "Global State of Democracy GSoD Index"[1], developed by International IDEA, "measures" democracy by the following five main attributes, concretized by 16 subattributes:

- **Representative government** (clean elections, inclusive suffrage, peaceful transfer of power, free political parties, elected government)
- **Fundamental rights** (access to justice, civil liberties, social rights, and equality)
- **Participatory engagement** (civil society participation, electoral participation, direct democracy, local democracy)
- **Impartial administration** (predictable enforcement of laws and decisions, absence of corruption)
- **Checks on government** (effective parliament, judicial independence, media integrity)

In a democratic system, these five elements are closely interrelated. However, perceptions of their content and relevance may differ considerably in practice, and the relations between the various aspects are not always without ambiguity. Principles of good governance are closely linked to democracy, such as transparency, equality, inclusion, individual freedom, respect for human rights, the rule of law, respon-

---

[1] https://www.idea.int/data-tools/tools/global-state-democracy-indices.

siveness, accountability, and checks and balances. For example, in the 12 Principles of Good Democratic Governance adopted by the Council of Europe in 2008 and targeting local authorities, both concepts are intertwined.[2] The operational functionality of state institutions that fulfill their tasks and provide public services in a responsive, effective, and efficient way is often assumed to be an intrinsic part of a democracy. Power-sharing as well as checks and balances play an important role in avoiding the abuse of power and increasing political stability, but these concepts may also foster powerful elites in their steering of political processes.[3] Fundamental rights and liberties, particularly freedom of expression, are perceived as fundamental for any democratic system. Finally, the views differ in how far democracy is a liberal concept of a rather formal equality of citizens, focusing on political institutions and processes – or whether democracy itself is intrinsically oriented towards social equality and the inclusion of all citizens in social, economic, and political life.

---

[2] https://rm.coe.int/12-principles-of-governance-poster-a2/1680787986.

[3] Bochsler, Daniel, and Juon, Andreas (2021). Power-sharing and the quality of democracy, European Political Science Review, 13, 411-430, with many references.

Democracy particularly depends on the quality of political processes such as elections, consultations, and participation, or collective agenda-setting and decision-making. The quality of these processes is closely linked to broader aspects such as political culture, the social environment, the history of the country at stake, individual and collective behaviors, and the mindsets of citizens and political actors. Respect for fundamental freedoms, particularly freedom of expression, the right and possibility to disagree, an individual critical mindset, the willingness to listen to and reflect on other opinions, and a sense of compromise are essential features favoring democratic processes. Lastly, the willingness to accept defeat – if it is the result of a legitimate and democratic decision-making process – is part of the political culture and mindset that are most relevant for the stability of democratic systems.

Two main questions are always present when discussing democracy. The first is about who is the "people", who should be entitled and empowered to participate as "citizens" in democratic systems, have a voice, be heard – and be part of the "demos". Women, poor people, migrants, vulnerable groups, or youth have often been systematically excluded for centuries and are still represented less effectively than men and powerful elites in political decision-making. In some countries, migrants do not have voting rights, even if their family has been living in that country for generations.

The second question concerns the way the will of the "people" should be elicited in a democracy. Often, both political powerholders and their opponents refer to the views of the "people" to justify their own positions, mirroring the fact that the "people" are far from being a homogenous body with a homogenous political will. When citizens or their representatives are divided on an issue, whose views and interests will prevail? What is to be considered a sufficient majority or majorities for legitimate decision-making? If majority rules are established, can (strong) minorities block the decisions on specific issues in specific cases and circumstances? Should the votes of certain groups or (territorial) associations be weighted specifically, or would, on the contrary, such an approach (protecting minorities) render decisions less democratic?

All this shows the multifaceted complexity of the concept of democracy: It is used daily by political actors in different contexts with changing content and priorities, and it is examined from different perspectives by numerous scholars with a variety of results and conclusions.

Why Do We Assume that Democracy is Desirable?

Political scientists mention a series of rationales for why democracy can be considered desirable compared to more authoritarian forms of government. It is assumed by many that:

- Democracy makes powerholders more accountable, preventing corruption and abuses of power.
- Democratic countries tend to be economically better off than autocratic systems and distribute wealth more equally.
- Democratic systems tend to make governments responsive to the needs of citizens and promote human development better than others – as measured by health, education, access to basic services, or access to rights and justice.
- Democracy helps people defend their own fundamental interests in political decision-making, protects their rights and personal freedoms, and provides space for citizens to make their own choices and decisions.
- Democracy contributes to balancing interests and preventing violent conflicts, both internally and internationally.

Do these assumptions hold true in reality? The realities are multicolored and complex. Context-specific evidence on the impact, success, and failure of democracy (or authoritarian systems) is difficult to identify. Firstly, scientific analyses of the effects and results of democratic systems are often based on differing concepts of democracy; thus, the state of democracy or autocracy is assessed differently. Secondly, the economic, social, or political criteria for measuring success and failure (or democracy dividends) may also differ considerably. Thirdly, it is difficult to measure the impact of political systems on economic and social dynamics as they are highly interdependent and do not follow a linear logic of cause and effect. Generally, "democracy" is not a panacea for good results in economic and social development, inclusion, or the peaceful management of political conflicts. Rather, the context – the specific institutional set-up, the political history and culture, the current political and social dynamics, and the economic and social environment – influences the way democratic principles are put into practice and determines the success of a democratic system. Moreover, the failure of a specific democratic system cannot be considered as evidence for the failure of democracy *per se*.

Nevertheless, a "democracy dividend" seems to be paying off in many aspects of economic and social development, including innovation and science, compared to authoritative systems.

For example, the V-DEM report 2022[4] makes a clear case for democracy by showing evidence from a variety of quantitative data and qualitative studies. Accordingly, democracy has a positive impact on a series of Sustainable Development Goals, such as economic growth, education, health, the management of climate change, gender equality, peace, and human security, the management of public goods, and fighting corruption. The report further states that the positive impacts of democracy are strongly linked to functional accountability mechanisms that are shaped by regular and transparent elections as well as by freedom of expression.

Assuming that democracy is indeed a concept to promote for a variety of economic, political, and social reasons, the question remains how that could be done best in international cooperation.

What Can International Cooperation Do to Support Democracy?

In the 1990s, the international trend towards democracy and respect for human rights was perceived by many political observers as well as

---

[4] https://v-dem.net/media/publications/dr_2022.pdf; with references to most recent analysis.

scientists as unavoidable. Many (Western) governments and international and regional organizations started to include bilateral and multilateral support for democratic reforms in their agenda of international cooperation and technical assistance.

One of the entry points for international actors supporting and consolidating democracy focused on strengthening the **multilateral framework** and its ability to set democratic standards and hold political power accountable. For example, coming out of Cold War times, the Organization of Security and Cooperation in Europe (OSCE) developed important standards for democratic elections, respect for human rights, freedom of the media, and the treatment of minorities, and elaborated and standardized international monitoring mechanisms, particularly in the field of elections. International and regional accountability frameworks on human rights provide different legal and political mechanisms for ensuring the respect of human rights and fundamental freedoms. They are used by international actors, local human rights defenders, and/or political actors to ask for respect for human rights obligations and challenge current powerholders and their undemocratic behavior. Although there is neither an international consensus on governance standards nor a common understanding of "democracy", the adoption of the 2030 Agenda for Sustainable Development[5] by the UN Sustainable Development Summit in 2015 was, at least partly, a success in recognizing globally that some democratic elements are key for sustainable development. The SDG 16, specifically, makes promoting peaceful and inclusive societies, access to justice for all, and building effective, accountable, and inclusive institutions an independent goal of development efforts at national and international levels.

At the same time, **bilateral relations** between many countries have been engaged in efforts to promote democracy, often in close cooperation with regional and international structures and processes, using the quality standards that were developed at the multilateral level. Promotional efforts addressed and continue to address a wide array of topics and themes relating to a variety of stakeholders, including election processes, constitutional and legal reforms, human rights, support for parliaments, the judiciary, government, and administration, strengthening accountability institutions (such as financial auditing institutions or human rights institutions), political parties, media, civil society, and human rights organizations. Supporting the inclusion and par-

---

[5] https://sdgs.un.org/goals.

ticipation of women in political processes was also a key priority.

A systemic perspective suggests that political systems are determined by three dimensions of a triangle: (1) political structures (legal framework, institutional structures, and resources); (2) political processes; and (3) the behavior of key stakeholders (political leaders, government representatives, judges, government officials, citizens, associations defending public or private interests, media, NGOs, etc.).

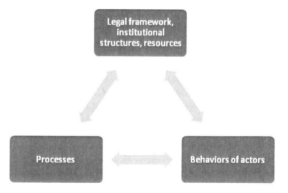

The success of democratic change will depend on the dynamics in all three dimensions – and between them. The promotion of democracy cannot be expected to be successful if it exclusively focuses on one dimension without considering the others. Nevertheless, looking at the three systemic dimensions helps clarify the various strategies and entry points that the promotion of democracy has used over the last thirty years.

Democratizing individual behavior of key stakeholders: In intergovernmental relations, diplomatic exchange and dialog often address this vector. Convincing or even pressuring powerholders in government to build political willingness for democratic change and to behave and act more democratically or supporting and empowering the drivers of democratic change in society are key strategies of democracy promotion. Other support actions focus not only on convincing but also on training, building technical capacities, and creating incentives for government officials, parliamentarians, law enforcement personnel, media actors, political party members, civil society groups, and human rights organizations to play their political roles in a competent and democratic way.

Democratizing political processes of decision-making: The support and monitoring of election processes have been a key entry point for international democracy promotion since the 90s. However, improving the quality of political decision-making processes was and is often also at the core of support for the government and administration, to make them more rule- and evidence-based as well as more transparent, effective, and efficient, often aiming to establish principles of consultation, compromise, and power-sharing. International support for parliaments in making their working processes more transparent, inclusive, and participatory, with a view to enabling the parliament's accountability function, was also at the heart of many interventions in favor of democratic change. Support for judicial reforms often focuses on new judicial proceedings that better respect the key features of the rule of law and human rights and improve the impact of the judiciary and law enforcement on the accountability of power holders.

Democratizing legal frameworks and institutional structures: Technical and/or financial support for legal and constitutional reforms were and are important entry points for democracy promotion, aiming to lay the legal and institutional foundations for democratic change. Support for electoral reforms includes new legal frameworks and institutional setups intended to guarantee free and fair electoral processes. By creating or allowing for new power centers, structural and administrative reforms such as decentralization have helped orient state structures more towards power-sharing, citizen participation, and compromise. Administrative reforms have established new institutional capacities in many public sectors, to respond to the needs of citizens and provide public services, sometimes specifically focusing on participatory approaches for decision-making. Building judicial and law enforcement structures and creating and strengthening oversight and accountability institutions were and are on the agenda of democracy support of many donors.

Good and Bad Practices in Promoting Democracy

Experience has shown that promoting democracy comes with a series of key risks that should be avoided or mitigated. They include, for example:

- Cut-and-paste approaches, blueprints, or generic solutions will not be successful. Inflexible and generic terminology that does not take into account local contextual factors will also not be helpful.
- Support for top-down approaches for implementing democratic reforms might not be very successful, as they might not be able to create a democratic culture that is sustainable and based on bottom-up participation.
- The funding of non-democratic actors or national actors that lack political legitimacy for

the task they are expected to perform may not bring good results, independent of the quality of the funded reform.
- Donors often bring a variety of ideas and concepts on how to implement democracy, often with no coordination among themselves, the risk of contradiction, confusion about the local purposes of reform, and frustration among partners, with the result of suffocating positive local dynamics.
- The aid industry, often working with the same implementation partners over the years, tends to build international expertise instead of local capacities and risks feeding into ODA business instead of driving change.
- Democracy promotion has often used ways and means that were not successful in the context at stake. But despite the evidence, democracy promotors were not always willing to learn and adapt, and outdated concepts and approaches are often still in use.
- Conditional approaches, which make financial or economic support dependent on democratic performance, are generally not perceived as beneficial for sustainable change.

On the other hand, experience has also shown good practices, including the following elements:

International Cooperation Promotes Democracy

- Understanding and adapting to the local context are very relevant dimensions for success at various levels: Understanding the local dynamics, respect for the local political systems and (legitimate) stakeholders, as well as local culture, working with local driving forces as partners and listening to them, adapting the democracy message to the needs, priorities, and terminology of the local context, and responding to local demand (instead of offering standardized solutions).
- Being transparent about the purpose, objectives, and measures of democracy promotion is important. Democracy promotion may be viewed critically by various actors in the target countries if the agenda of self-interest of the promoter is hidden. To avoid detrimental effects on the donor's own legitimacy and credibility – and those of its local partners – open communication with local actors and cooperation with other donors are key.
- Long-term commitment to democracy should be coupled with short-term flexibility in the selection of means. Adapting strategies, entry points and partnerships to rapidly changing circumstances is crucial.
- Policy instruments, political dialogue, and technical and financial instruments for promoting democracy should be systematically

combined. In addition, other areas such as trade and business, peace, and security should also be involved in more coherent and broad policies of democracy promotion.
- The reference to international and regional standards and corresponding international obligations (in the fields of election and human rights, but also in anti-corruption, trade, and climate change) can be used for legitimizing democracy promotion in different ways and across a variety of topics.

What Were the Results of International Efforts?

The last decade has shown that the considerable international effort to promote democracy in specific contexts has given mixed results at best (for a deeper analysis, see the chapter by Richard Youngs in this volume). Various analyses provide evidence that authoritarian regimes are on the rise.[6]

---

[6] See, among others, the most recent report of International IDEA, Global State of Democracy 2022: Forging Social Contracts in a Time of Discontent; and The Global State of Democracy 2021: Building Resilience in a Pandemic Era (idea.int); The V-DEM's democracy report 2022, https://v-dem.net/media/publications/dr_2022.pdf.

For example, according to the V-Dem's Democracy Report 2022, the level of democracy enjoyed by the average global citizen in 2021 is down to 1989 levels. It concludes that dictatorships are on the rise and harbor 70% of the world's population. Evidence of a democratic decline is observed particularly in the Asia-Pacific region, Eastern Europe, and Central Asia, as well as in parts of Latin America and the Caribbean. The "electoral autocracy" remains the most common type of regime in the world. So-called toxic polarization emerged while respect for political counterarguments and associated aspects of the deliberative component of democracy worsened in more than 32 countries compared to 2011. The year 2021 saw the highest number of nations autocratizing in the last 50 years.

The Democracy Report 2022 also states that across regions, elections are the aspect of democracy with the highest improvement among democratizing states. On the other hand, across regions, repression of civil society worsened in 2022 and censorship of the media in 21 of the 33 autocratizing countries. Popular mobilization for democracy continues to stay at low levels and risks allowing autocratization to deepen unchallenged. The report suggests that this may contribute to the fact that bolder actions of autocratization are becoming more common. The report finally confirms that governments increasingly use misinformation to shape domestic and international opinion.

It is difficult to assess how far international democracy promotion slowed the trend towards autocratization, had a decisive impact, or perhaps even contributed to the negative dynamics that we observe today. In any case, international democracy promotion is confronted with both old and new challenges, including the rapidly growing digitalization of the public space and the great risk of global and local disinformation and manipulation (see the chapter by Idayat Hassan in this volume). Authoritarian regimes have been resistant to the frequently increasing democratic demands of their own citizens by directly using repressive means or by circumventing the democratic rules of the game. International promotion of democracy becomes highly sensitive in such circumstances. If it is not covered by international obligations, it might be rejected by powerholders with the argument of unlawful interference in internal affairs. Promoting democracy may even risk delegitimizing and weakening national driving forces for democracy – and finally do harm. International support for democratic reforms has also been criticized for being insufficiently sensitive to the context, the political economy, and the cultural background of the targeted countries, or for self-interested motivations, hidden agendas, or incoherent approaches, and finally for poor coordination among international actors.

To conclude, the debate about democracy and international democracy promotion seems to have gained in importance and political attention in the most recent times of crisis. Many questions need further and continuous reflection, such as: What is the purpose of promoting democracy, in this increasingly challenging context? How important is the objective of democracy promotion among other objectives of bilateral and multilateral policy? What works best for promoting democracy in authoritarian contexts? What role do authoritarian states (and their financial support as international donors) play in strengthening other authoritarian regimes – and weakening or even discrediting democracy? How do political trends in our own democracies (such as toxic polarization, declining confidence in, and even obstructing political processes and institutions) impact international democracy promotion?

About the Author

Dr. Erika Schläppi is an attorney at law by training. She has been working as an independent consultant since 1998, based in Bern, Switzerland, specializing in the fields of democratic governance and the rule of law, international human rights (including women's rights and gender), and development cooperation. She provides expert support, advice, capacity building, and training to a variety of stakeholders in different roles, working in a variety of institutional and cultural contexts. Erika Schläppi co-founded the Ximpulse consultancy team in 2009 (www.ximpulse.ch), working on governance, political analysis, power-sharing, and multilayer processes mainly in developing and transition countries, often in conflict or post-conflict situations.

Selected Bibliography

Boese, Vanessa Alexandra, Gates, Scott, Knutsen, Carl Henrik, Nygard, Håvard Mokleiv, and Strand, Havard (2022). "Patterns of Democracy over Space and Time". International Studies Quarterly. 66(3) 1-19, https://doi.org/10.1093/isq/sqac041.

Carothers, Thomas (2015). Democracy aid at 25: Time to Choose. Journal of Democracy, 26(1), pp. 59-73.

Carothers, Thomas, and Saskia Brechenmacher (2014). "Closing Space: Democracy and Human Rights Support Under Fire", Carnegie Endowment for International Peace (2014).

European Partnership for Democracy EPD. (2018). European Union democracy assistance: An academic state of play, https://epd.eu/wp-content/uploads/2018/12/EU-Democracy-Assistance.pdf.

Gafuri, Adea (2021). "Can democracy aid improve democracy? The European Union's democracy assistance 2002 – 2018". Democratization, DOI: https://doi.org/10.1080/13510347.2021.2012654.

Gerring, John, Knutsen, Carl Henrik, Berge, Jonas (2022). "Does Democracy Matter?" Annual Review Political Science. 25:357-75. https://doi.org/10.1146/annurev-polisci-060820-060910.

Ghardallou, W., Sridi, D. (2020). "Democracy and Economic Growth: A Literature Review". J Knowl Econ 11, 982–1002. https://doi.org/10.1007/s13132-019-00594-4.

Gjelow, Haakon, Knutsen, Carl Henrik, Wig, Tore and Wilson, Matthew Charles (2021). "One Road to Riches? How State Building and Democratization Affect Economic Development". Cambridge. Cambridge University Press, Riches? How State Building and Democratization Affect Economic Development". Cambridge: Cambridge University Press, https://www.cambridge.org/core/elements/abs/one-road-toriches/67E7EF36A37E7881168B1E145F78B8.

Hobson, C. and Kurki, M. (eds.) (2012). The conceptual politics of democracy promotion. London: Routledge.

International IDEA, "Democracy and Peacebuilding in the Framework of SDG 16+", Policy Recommendations from an Interregional and Multistakeholder Approach, International IDEA Discussion Paper 1/2020.

John Gerring, Knutsen, Carl Henrik, Maguire, Matthew Maguire, Skaaning, Svend-Erik, Teorell, Jan & Coppedge, Michael (2021). "Democracy and human development: issues of conceptualization and measurement", Democratization, 28:2, 308-332, DOI: 10.1080/13510347.2020.1818721.

Ruth-Lovell, Saskia Pauline, and Grahn, Sandra (2022). "Threat or corrective to democracy? The relationship between populism and different models of democracy". European Journal of Political Research. https://doi.org/10.1111/1475-6765.12564.

Wetzel, A., Orbie, J. & Bossuyt, F. (2017). Comparative perspectives on EU Democracy Promotion. London: Routledge.

Youngs, Richard (2015). "The Puzzle of Non-Western Democracies", Carnegie Endowment for International Peace.

Selected Websites

Carnegie Europe, The European Democracy hub, https://carnegieeurope.eu/specialprojects/EuropeanDemocracyHub/.

International IDEA, International Institution for Democracy and Electoral Assistance, https://www.idea.int.

OSCE Office for democratic institutions and human rights ODIHR, https://www.osce.org/odihr.

The Council of Europe's platform on democracy, https://www.coe.int/en/web/compass/democracy.

UN platform for accessing information on democracy, https://www.un.org/en/global-issues/democracy.

V-DEM Varieties of Democracy, https://v-dem.net/about/.

Supporting Democracy – Of, By, and For the People

Matching International and National Government Assistance with Local and Non-Governmental Efforts is the Order of the Hour

Bruno KAUFMANN

In the darkest hours of the 20th century, Thomas Mann, the Nobel Prize-winning author of the saga *Buddenbrooks: The Decline of a Family*, made a strong statement against fascist regimes in Europe and beyond.

"Democracy will win", he declared from his American exile, because it can be renewed by the participation of citizens. "Democracy is timelessly human, and timelessness always implies a certain amount of potential youthfulness".

Mann, who was born in Lübeck in 1875 and would die in Zurich in 1955, would use his personal journey – from a convinced monarchist skeptical about the benefits of modern democracy to a stringent supporter of genuine people power – to answer the devastation of World

War II and the Holocaust with a call for "Democracy First"[1].

Thomas Mann's insights appeared then to be anti-factual, with an inhuman and antidemocratic catastrophe unfolding. Even so, Mann's words drew from the advances during democracy's early 20th century rollercoaster ride – including the breakthrough of universal suffrage in many countries. Moreover, Mann's insights paved the way for the building of a new foundation of global cooperation and human rights after the collapse of fascist regimes in 1945.

The end of the war did not end attacks against democracy; democracy is always under assault and always questioned, especially in the last 70 years. Democracy often advances and declines at the same time. The establishment of better practices, innovative democratic tools, and new democratic rights coincides with attempts to undermine freedoms, cancel election results, and start wars against developing democracies. One such war, Russia's attack against its neighbor

---

[1] A series of books, exhibitions, and events have been organized since 2018 – 80 years after the famous speech – in Europe and across the United States. Frido Mann, the grandchild of the author, has also published a book in German with this quote ("Democracy will win – Bekenntnisse eines Weltbürgers") and has shared his findings.

Ukraine, arrives now on top of other crises, including the pandemic and climate change, which have put democracy under higher pressure.

If democracy is declining now, it is declining from a high mark. After the fall of the Berlin Wall in 1989 and the end of the Cold War, democracy advanced around the world. A peak was reached in 2012, with 42 countries being declared by Freedom House to be "full democracies", while today just 34 such countries remain home to only 13% of the world population. On the other side of the spectrum, the number of "closed autocracies" increased in the last ten years from 25 to 30 countries. In between, there are more than 100 hybrid societies, experiencing a constant struggle between free and unfree, democracy and autocracy[2].

This struggle for the middle ground deserves more attention. In this century, major powers, including China, Russia, and to some extent also India and the United States, have turned from democratizing to autocratizing, with huge neg-

---

[2] For a full overview of the state of democracy a growing number of institutions and organizations are providing research results, assessments, and information including the "Varieties of Democracy"-institute at the University of Gothenburg of Sweden, which publishes an annual report: https://v-dem.net/media/publications/dr_2022.pdf.

ative implications for the international order. In response, medium-sized and smaller countries, as well as international organizations, the media, academia, and civil societies, have come together in mutual recognition that the development of democracy needs much more care, effort, and investment. This undeclared league of democracy saw that democracy and their democratic societies would be strained by future global crises.

This democratic league has championed new ways to involve everyday people in governance (for example, through participatory budgeting) and inspired pro-democratic thinking from the local level to the transnational level. Examples of this democratic work can be seen in the United Nations declaration of an International Day of Democracy (September 15)[3] and in the introduction of the first tool of transnational participatory and direct democracy, the European Citizens' Initiative (fully operational in 2012)[4].

In two ways, these developments in the UN and within the European Union are critical to the new method of democracy support: First, both UN Democracy Day and the EU Citizens Initiative (ECI) originated outside of government, as

---

[3] https://www.un.org/en/observances/democracy-day.
[4] https://europa.eu/citizens-initiative/_en.

civil society initiatives, in the early 1990s[5]. Second, both developments have created transnational umbrellas for new civic society activities and proposals, allowing active citizens around the world to bring their democratic contribution forward. In the case of the European Union, the ECI allows even smaller groups of people to formally enter the pan-European process of agenda-setting and decision-making supported by an EU infrastructure, offering advice and free translation services into all 23 official languages.

While classical international development work for decades has benefited from government and non-governmental cooperation, democracy support until recently has been hampered by sinkhole thinking. Every stakeholder did their own thing, pairing together similarly minded actors (like political parties, trade Unions, or sports clubs, even twin cities) and thus reinforcing the limitations of each initiative to reach and persuade people. Only recently have national governments and NGOs begun to understand that efficient democracy needs a much more multi-dimensional approach – because, as the scholar Larry Diamond put it in *Foreign Affairs*, "All Democracy Is Global"[6].

---

[5] https://www.democracy.community/stories/challenging-making-european-citizens-initiative.

[6] "All Democracy Is Global – Why America Can't Shrink

The notion that all local democracy is global and that all global democracy is local was the founding idea behind the "Global Forum on Modern Direct Democracy", established in 2008.

I know because I, a veteran journalist and foreign correspondent for the Swiss Broadcasting Company, was its founder. Starting the Global Forum continued work that had begun for me in the late 1980s when I went to the Baltic States to report on and assess the (un)making of democratic principles, procedures, and practices. Ever since I have been traveling the world continuously to report on democracy and to compare notes with journalist colleagues in every corner of the world. On one of those many fact-finding trips, I sat in then-California Governor Arnold Schwarzenegger's office in Sacramento. Here I met my Californian "alter ego" Joe Mathews, an experienced reporter of democracy in the Golden State and across the United States, who was writing a book about the Austrian Terminator. And we started the Global Forum, our never-ending and constantly expanding conversation on how to make democracy more democratic.

---

from the Fight for Freedom". In Foreign Affairs, the Age of Uncertainty, September/October 2022 issue.

In fact, we invited the world of civic democracy supporters to these conversations, and many came and engaged. After the first edition of the Global Forum in Aarau/Switzerland in October 2008, worldwide gatherings were organized in places as geographically well-distributed and culturally diverse as Seoul, Korea (2009), San Francisco, US (2010), Montevideo, Uruguay (2012), Tunis, Tunisia (2015), San Sebastian, Spain (2016), Rome, Italy (2018), Taichung, Taiwan (2019), Lucerne, Switzerland (2022), and Mexico City (2023).

At each of these eleven world conferences, gathering typically between 500 and 1000 democracy supporters from up to 100 countries, we heard from people from all walks of life, most of whom had engaged locally first. The very diverse local contexts of our Forum settings heavily influenced and enriched the conversations and works of the participants.

In Korea, the internal divide and conflict-prone situation were the pretext for a strong democratization drive by civil society in the South. In Montevideo, the paramount role of political parties in Uruguayan democracy offered new insights into the interplay of indirect and direct democracy. At the Global Forum in Tunis, the cooperation amongst the Dialogue Quartet (which later that year won the Nobel Peace Prize) was a powerful reminder that strong religious beliefs and traditions are able to coexist with modern democratic ways of life.

At the 2022 Forum in Lucerne, Switzerland, it became clear that, as the participants concluded in their official declaration[7], "time may not be on democracy's side. We conclude our forum with a fierce urgency to defend and extend democracy right now, in service of a greater future". The worldwide coronavirus pandemic, the intensification of the climate emergency, and the unprovoked war by the world's biggest country against Europe's biggest democracy dominated the five days of discussion by more than 650 democracy experts and supporters from more than 50 countries worldwide.

The "fierce urgency" to act on behalf of democracy could be felt throughout the forum. Swiss government representatives committed to following the nation's constitutional duties to "support democracy globally". Civil society organizations and activists from six continents proposed ways to make democracy more demo-

---

[7] The Lucerne Declaration on Modern Direct Democracy: https://www.democracy.community/files/inline-files/the_lucerne_declaration_on_modern_democracy.pdf.

cratic and participatory. And at the Democracy City Summit that concluded the forum, local representatives from several cities signed the "Magna Charta for an International League of Democracy Cities".

The Lucerne Declaration ended with these formulations:

We have many disagreements – which is good because disagreement is central to democracy! But we also had a strong, shared sense that we need to change how the world thinks about democracy. Put simply, democracy should always be thought of, evaluated, and developed from the bottom up. To survive and grow, democracy and its friends must focus on empowering everyday people. And the powers of democratic citizens must involve much more than voting for representatives. We the people must have the right to make our laws, to develop our plans, and to change our constitutions. In other words, the people of the world have the right to govern themselves, directly.[8]

Out of these rich and diverse exchanges over 15 years of Global Forums, we have identified new opportunities for democracy. These opportunities depend on a new and post-paternalistic structure for national governments and inter-

---

[8] Ibid.

national governmental organizations to partner with non-governmental organizations and stakeholders in several ways.

(1) Establishing strong non-state platforms for democracy promotion and support

In 1952, Germany established the Federal Agency for Homeland Services (renamed in 1963 the Federal Agency for Civic Education) to educate the German people about democratic principles and prevent any moves to re-establish a totalitarian regime. It was the first such institution to focus on finding lessons from the tumultuous history of democracy to seek to avoid backsliding and the return to non-democratic regimes.

In the 1980s, Korea[9] and Taiwan[10], two host countries of the Global Forum, established "Democracy Foundations" as they transitioned away from military rule and non-democratic government. These state-launched foundations have thrived, honoring the memory and achievements of domestic democracy movements, investing heavily in democracy education (following the example of the German party founda-

---
[9] www.kdemo.or.kr/en/.
[10] www.tfd.org.tw/opencms/english/.

tions), and becoming international partners of democracy supporters across the world.

While the structure of bi-partisan government control ensured basic resources and professional continuity in these two Asian democratic tigers, politics also created many challenges to these foundations, especially when it came to cooperation with non-governmental and international stakeholders.

As a consequence, Global Forum partners in 2016 established the non-governmental Swiss Democracy Foundation[11] (SDF) as a new cooperative platform for global democracy assistance based in the heart of Europe. SDF has become an important hub, combining an "internal" focus on youth power and democracy education within the country with "external" efforts to assist global projects (some of which are described below).

The SDF cooperates with partners in Switzerland, Europe, and around the globe. Among them are multistakeholder platforms like Participedia[12], PeoplePowered[13], and the Participatory

---

[11] https://www.swissdemocracy.foundation/index.php/start.
[12] https://participedia.net/.
[13] https://www.peoplepowered.org/.

Budgeting World Atlas[14]. At the 2022 Global Forum on Modern Direct Democracy, the SDF partnered with more than 40 Swiss and international entities, including government partners like the Federal Ministry of Foreign Affairs in Switzerland[15], under which the 2022 Global Forum was part of the "Summit4Democracy" pledge program[16].

Establishing and supporting strong non-state platforms for democracy – such as the Swiss Democracy Foundation and other international and national non-governmental organizations – should become a more frequent strategy for building bridges between representative governments and citizens at all political levels.

---

[14] https://www.pbatlas.net/

[15] https://www.state.gov/wp-content/uploads/2022/04/SWITZERLAND-Summit-for-Democracy-Accessible-412022.pdf.

[16] "Unpacking the Summit for Democracy Commitments", International IDEA (2022), https://www.idea.int/sites/default/files/publications/unpacking-summit-for-democracy-commitments.pdf.

(2) Supporting research designed to assist not only further research but also practitioners in politics, administration, media and civil society

In spring 2021, almost 100 million citizens were called to a popular vote on the revocation of their head of state in Mexico[17]. It was a historic first. A few months earlier, the Mexicans – in another first – were invited to make up their minds and vote on a proposal to punish former presidents for corruption[18]. In both cases, less than 20 percent of the eligible voters participated, hence invalidating the decision, which required a minimum turnout of 40% to be valid. As a consequence, researchers and observers discussed the structure and context of the two first Mexican attempts at direct democracy[19].

The growing legal existence and practical use of participatory and direct democratic mechanisms have become a major new field of international research in recent years. How these tools are structured legally, how they function in practice, and how they develop democracy are all questions being examined by a growing community

---

[17] www.ine.mx/revocacion-mandato/.
[18] www.ine.mx/consultapopular/.
[19] www.swissinfo.ch/eng/recall-vote--mexico-uses-a-swiss-democracy-tool/47499008.

of research institutions and centers around the world.

These developments mirror the continuous extension of citizen-centered practices at all political levels in recent years. These changes also provide a response to the legitimacy crisis of representative electoral governments, which too often fail to offer genuine political participation, transparency, and democratic accountability at all levels of government action, including the transnational.[20]

Of course, new mechanisms that bring more people into political participation and democracy create new challenges. More direct democratic mechanisms can have powerful impacts. Both skeptics and friends of direct citizen democracy refer to the 2016 UK decision to "Leave the European Union" as an example of how "not to use direct democracy"[21]. But there is agreement among researchers and close observers that the effects of citizen decision-making depend heav-

---

[20] This is not a new insight: https://carnegieendowment.org/2014/10/20/accountability-transparency-participation-and-inclusion-new-development-consensus-pub-56968.

[21] One such voice is the former Swiss President Kaspar Villiger: https://www.swissinfo.ch/eng/directdemocracy/swiss-criticism_-the-brexit-vote-wasn-t-direct-democracy--it-was-drivel-/44155278.

ily on the specific construction of democratic procedures. So, it is essential that we better understand the often-complex rules of, for example, citizens' initiative procedures, popular referendums, and citizens' assemblies.

A novel and vital research process around the legal designs of direct democratic mechanisms started in the early 2010s at the Bergische University of Wuppertal in Germany. That was previously the home of a database for initiatives and referendums on the local and regional level within Germany[22]. A decade ago, that database went global. The research effort has created an internationally developed typology of modern DD mechanisms called the "Direct Democracy Navigator",[23] which has become the world's premier database in the field. The Navigator is now hosted by the Liechtenstein Institute in Bendern[24] and has been funded by both Swiss and non-Swiss institutions and organizations[25].

---

[22] idpf.uni-wuppertal.de/de/.
[23] www.direct-democracy-navigator.org.
[24] www.liechtenstein-institut.li/forschungsbereiche/direkte-demokratie.
[25] Among the historic funders you find the Swiss Federal Chancellery and SWI swissinfo.ch. Currently the Navigator is mainly co-financed by Democracy International and the Swiss Democracy Foundation.

The knowledge and findings in the "Direct Democracy Navigator" have been instrumental in civic education efforts like the "Global Passport to Modern Direct Democracy"[26], "The European Democracy Passport"[27], and the "Swiss Democracy Passport"[28]. Now the "Navigator" must extend its outreach in order to inform and educate designers and practitioners of modern direct democracy. The Navigator should be part of any research support initiatives and programs.

(3) Inspiring worldwide efforts for strong subnational governments to efficiently practice and innovate democracy from below

The conventional wisdom is that electoral democracy is in decline.[29] But this ignores another widespread trend: Direct democracy at the local and regional level is booming, even as disillusion with representative government at the national level grows.

---

[26] www.idea.int/publications/catalogue/global-passport-modern-direct-democracy.
[27] www.eesc.europa.eu/en/our-work/publications-other-work/publications/european-democracy-passport.
[28] https://www.swissinfo.ch/eng/politics/recall-vote--mexico-uses-a-swiss-democracy-tool/47499008.
[29] www.v-dem.net/publications/democracy-reports/.

Today, 113 of the world's countries offer their citizens legally or constitutionally established rights to bring forward a citizens' initiative, a referendum, or both. And since 1980, roughly 80 percent of countries worldwide[30] have had at least one nationwide referendum or popular vote on a legislative or constitutional issue.

Indeed, there are two main trends – the rise of populist authoritarianism in some nations and the rise of local and direct democracy in some areas – and they are related. Frustration is growing with democratic systems at national levels, and yes, some people become more attracted to populism. But some of that frustration is channeled into positive energy – into making local democracy more democratic and direct.

Cities from Seoul to San Francisco are hungry for new and innovative tools that bring citizens into processes of deliberation that allow the people themselves to make decisions and feel invested in government actions. We've seen local governments embrace participatory budgeting, participatory planning, citizens' juries, and a host of experimental digital tools in service of that desired mix of greater public deliberation and more direct public action.

---

[30] www.idea.int/data-tools/question-view/482.

At the 2018 Global Forum in Rome, Italy, dozens of city representatives from across the world developed the original draft of a "Magna Charta for an International League of Democracy Cities". This document[31], which has been amended and rewritten since then by everyday people around the world, identifies 20 different dimensions for democratic progress on the local level so that citizens and urban institutions can form an idea of where their own cities rank in terms of democracy development.

And this is far from the only global initiative to connect local governments around the world on the issue of democratic innovation, participation, and support. The democratic issues are also very much present and supported in organizations like the Barcelona-based United Cities and Local Governments[32], the Vienna-headquartered European Capital of Democracy project,[33] or the US-hosted Democracy Cities network[34].

Around the world, we are seeing cooperation between new, democracy-focused media projects that often operate on local or sub-national levels. To assist this work and to expand reporting on

---

[31] www.democracy.community/stories/magna-charta.
[32] www.uclg.org/en/organisation/about.
[33] capitalofdemocracy.eu.
[34] www.democracycities.org/why.

and knowledge of local democracy, we are building a new global media platform for democracy, devoted to democratic ideas and stories from the local level.

Using our Global Forum network, we hope to connect the world's many democratic efforts more closely with local citizens and governments. The goal is to build a network of networks to support efficient democratic practice and innovative democratic approaches in the future.

(4) Highlighting and assisting electoral management bodies and networks globally to ensure the free and fair conduct of elections – and also the trustworthy administration of democratic tools and participatory processes.

The most recent series of highly contested elections and referendums in late 2022 offered a state of the art in electoral integrity – and the art of conceding. One of the more impressive election night speeches during the so-called midterm elections in the United States was delivered by Tim Ryan in the state of Ohio. The Democratic candidate lost the Senate race against Republican J.D. Vance and said: "I have a privilege right now … to concede this race … because the way this country operates is that, when you lose an election, you concede and you respect the will of the people".[35]

What should be the most normal way of dealing with a loss at the ballot box has, in recent years, increasingly been challenged. Most notably is the unwillingness of former US president Donald Trump to concede in the 2020 election – an election that by the American Cybersecurity and Infrastructure Security Agency (CISA) was labeled as "most secure in American history"[36].

Despite this assessment and his obvious defeat, Trump nonetheless continued to claim that the election was "stolen from him", leading up to the January 6, 2021, attack on the US Capitol building by his supporters. This resulted in the deaths of six people and injuries to over 130 police officials.

These "big lie" campaigns across the US have inspired a wave of similar campaigns to play the "stolen election" card in the Americas, in Europe, and around the world. So, there was lit-

---

[35] eu.usatoday.com/story/opinion/contributors/2022/11/09/midterm-elections-concede-race-graciously-win/8313925001/.
[36] https://www.cisa.gov/news/2020/11/12/joint-statement-elections-infrastructure-government-coordinating-council-election.

tle surprise when extremist supporters of former Brazil president Jair Bolsonaro (who lost the presidential elections in his country) on January 9, 2023, replicated the January 6 insurrection by storming the Brazilian Congress, Supreme Court, and presidential palace, requesting the military abolish democracy.

In response to this international move of autocracy support, many organizations, including electoral management ones and non-partisan and non-governmental democracy groups, have started to strengthen the electoral process, paying closer attention to fake news and informing the public much more comprehensively and patiently about every step of the electoral process.

Still, the "big lie on stolen elections" theory is unlikely to disappear just by improving digital literacy and building more robust electoral institutions. In the US, a recent poll[37] showed that around half of Americans (53% among Republicans and 49% among Democrats) believe it is at least somewhat likely that in the next few years, officials will successfully overturn the results of a US election because their party did not win.

It will therefore be critical to further strengthen (independent) electoral management bodies

---

[37] edition.cnn.com/2022/07/21/politics/cnn-poll-elections/index.html.

around the world and support organizations and networks that, through their work, contribute to making electoral processes more robust, freer, and fairer.

Summing up, current developments and trends offer a clear choice between more democratic vs. more autocratic developments. The world is currently experiencing a wave of autocratization characterized by increasing executive power, erosion of democratic norms, and a general tendency toward less freedom. One-third of the world's population – 2.6 billion people – now lives in countries experiencing autocratization.

This is tragic because the most extensive study of data shows that democracy delivers better outcomes for people. Studies and data from the Varieties of Democracy institute at the University of Gothenburg have shown that democracy bests autocracy in areas like "Economic Development and Reducing Poverty"[38], "Education and Empowering Women"[39], "Peace and Human Security"[40], "Sustainable Environment and Climate Change Mitigation"[41] as well as "Human Devel-

---

[38] https://v-dem.net/media/publications/c4d_1_final_2.pdf.
[39] https://v-dem.net/media/publications/pb_28.pdf.
[40] https://v-dem.net/media/publications/pb30.pdf.
[41] https://v-dem.net/media/publications/pb_31.pdf.

opment and Global Health"[42]. In sum, democracy makes us richer, more equal, safer, healthier, and more sustainable than autocracy.

This positive assessment is mirrored by the global and broad support of most people for both representative government and forms of participatory and direct democracy. A survey by the Pew Research Center indicates that pro-democracy positions are clearly prevailing vis-à-vis preferences for autocratic forms of government. Accordingly, 78% of people in the 38 countries surveyed regard "representative democracy" as "good", while only 17% regard it as "bad". Asked about their stand for "direct democracy", 66% of people from these countries around the world have a positive stance, and 30% have a more "negative" one[43]. Asked about their "satisfaction" with the current workings of their democracies, only 44% think that the current democracies are good enough[44]

---

[42] https://v-dem.net/media/publications/pb_29.pdf.
[43] https://www.pewresearch.org/global/2017/10/16/globally-broad-support-for-representative-and-direct-democracy/.
[44] https://www.pewresearch.org/short-reads/2020/02/27/how-people-around-the-world-see-democracy-in-8-charts/.

About the Author

Bruno Kaufmann is the Global Democracy Correspondent at the Swiss Broadcasting Company. Born and raised in Switzerland he studied Peace- and Conflict Research at the Universities of Zurich (Switzerland), Göteborg (Sweden) and Honolulu (US). Between 2008 and 2023 Bruno Kaufmann co-chaired the Global Forum on Modern Direct Democracy and is board member of the Swiss Democracy Foundation. He lives with his family in Sweden and is the author of many publications including the "Global Passport to Modern Direct Democracy" and the "European Democracy Passport".

Literature

Transnationale Demokratie – Anstösse zu einem europäischen Verfassungsprozess, Realotopia (1995).

The Rostock Process. 1991-2004: On the Way to More Direct Democracy in Europe. Geschichtswerkstatt Rostock (2001).

The European Referendum Challenge. IRI Report on the growing importance of the initiative and referendum process in the European integration process. Amsterdam (2002).

Transnational Democracy in the Making. IRI Europe Handbook 2004. Amsterdam (2003).

Direct Democracy in Europe: A Comprehensive Reference Guide to the Initiative and Referendum Process in Europe. Carolina Academic Press. Durham (2004).

The European Constitution – Bringing in the People. European Parliament. Brussels (2004).

Guidebook to Direct Democracy – in Switzerland and beyond, 2005-10 Editions. IRI Europe. Brussels (2007). [available in 10 languages].

Initiative for Europe – your guide towards transnational democracy. Handbook 2008. Brussels (2007).

The European Citizens' Initiative Your Guide to the First Transnational Direct Democratic Tool in World History. By Bruno Kaufmann, with an introduction by Gerald Häfner. Green European Foundation. Brussels. (2010)

Mehr direkte Demokratie wagen. Handbuch zur Europäischen Bürgerinitiative. Eine Gebrauchsanweisung zur transnationalen, direkten Demokratie. (2011).

Transnational Citizens' Initiative – how modern direct democracy can make the European Union a better place for minorities, by Bruno Kaufmann in "Direct Democracy and Minorities", edited by Wilfried Marxer. Springer VS. (2012).

The Next Big Thing Making Europe ready for the Citizens' Initiative. Edited by Bruno Kaufmann and Johannes Pichler. Wissenschaftsverlag. (2012).

The European Citizens' Initiatives Into new democratic territory. Edited by Bruno Kaufmann and

Johannes Pichler. Wissenschaftsverlag, Berlin. (2012).

Transnational "Babystep" the European Citizens' Initiative, by Bruno Kaufmann in "Citizens' Initiatives in Europe", edited by Maja Setälä and Theo Schiller. Palgrave, Macmillan. (2012).

The European Citizens' Initiative Pocket Guide Green European Foundation, Brussels/Belgium. (2013) [available in 8 languages].

International Masters Curriculum for Electoral Administration on Participatory and Direct Democracy, United Nations Institute for Training and Research, Pisa. (2017).

The Guide to the European Citizens' Initiative, European Economic and Social Committee, Brussels/Belgium. (2014) [available in 23 languages].

European Passport to Active Citizenship, European Economic and Social Committee, Brussels/Belgium. (2015) [available in 23 languages].

Global Passport to Modern Direct Democracy, International Institute for Electoral and Democracy Support (IDEA), Stockholm. (2017) [available in 10 languages].

The European Democracy Passport, European Economic and Social Committee. (2021).

Swiss Democracy Passport, Swiss Foreign Ministry. (2022).

A Revival for International Democracy Support?

Richard YOUNGS

This chapter charts the overall evolution of international democracy support in the last thirty years. It describes how an initial period of expanding democracy-supporting commitments in the 1990s and early 2000s gave way to democratic retrenchment in the 2010s. In the last few years, the geopolitics of authoritarian assertiveness appears to be fostering a renewed commitment to defending and supporting democratic norms. The chapter concludes by suggesting how the Russian invasion of Ukraine will determine how this new momentum is taken forward.

Winds Change Direction

International democracy support took root in the era immediately after the Cold War, when the context was relatively benign and international efforts filtered into a global expansion of democratization processes. This favourable context began to shift in the late 2000s and the 2010s, when it became increasingly clear that an era of visceral geopolitics was taking shape in ways unfavourable to democracy. Russian and Chinese assertiveness have come to represent a constant annoyance and disruptive spoiler to those actors desiring more democratic forms of governance. A "multi-order" world emerged, and this made democracy support increasingly challenging.

Many analysts saw global geopolitics in terms of a declining "liberal democratic alliance" of Western states losing power to rising authoritarian states like China, Russia and Saudi Arabia. As the United States steps back from underwriting the liberal order, a "jungle" of clashing values and interests has begun to weaken commitment to democratic norms. As non-Western resistance gains ground, the place of democracy in international geopolitics and the global order has come under greater threat.

The global order seemed now to be working better for authoritarian regimes than democracies: Autocracies defend themselves from global liberal influences through blocking tactics and repression, but democracies cannot defend themselves from global illiberal-authoritarian influences.¹ Democracy seemed to be increasingly caught up negatively in global geopolitical rivalry. This has now moved into a further stage of "epochal confrontation" between power and legitimacy – a struggle that has moved from the realms of soft power to harder confrontation too.²

Defensive Reactions

As these geopolitical risks mounted, Western states were in retreat mode and made little effort to strengthen the defence of democracy against the authoritarian power surge. In most cases, they gradually pulled back from ambitious policies to support democracy around the world. Democratic powers outside the West gained influence but were relatively cautious in joining any broad international effort to defend democratic values.

International efforts to defend and extend democratic norms weakened over the 2010s. Some international cooperation took place in defence of democratic breakthroughs, for example, in

---

[1] A. Cooley and D. Nexon, The real crisis of global order: illiberalism on the rise, Foreign Affairs, Jan 2022.
[2] L. Diamond, Democracy's arc: From resurgent to imperilled, JD, Jan 2022.

Ukraine or in development-aid commitments around the Social Development Goals. But, overall, a more realpolitik tone became more apparent in international relations. Many talked of the need for a concert of great powers – one that recognised geopolitics as too important to be distracted by considerations of democracy.[3]

President Obama's foreign policy foregrounded pragmatism and realism, while being ideologically shaped by liberalism.[4] While the first Obama administration did engage in some democracy issues around the world, it also prioritized security and economic interests over these.[5] The US response to the Arab Spring was mixed, with support for democracy where political change occurred – in Tunisia, Egypt, Libya, Syria, and Yemen – but continued cooperation with resilient autocratic allies such as

---

[3] C. Kupchan and R. Hass (2021). Foreign Policy.
[4] Brendon O'Connor and Danny Cooper, "Ideology and the Foreign Policy and Barack Obama: A Liberal-Realist Approach to International Affairs", *Presidential Studies Quarterly* 51, no. 3 (2021): 635-666, https://doi.org/10.1111/psq.12730.
[5] Thomas Carothers, "Democracy Policy Under Obama: Revitalization or Retreat?", Carnegie Endowment for International Peace, January 11, 2012, https://carnegieendowment.org/2012/01/11/democracy-policy-under-obama-revitalization-or-retreat-pub-46443.

Bahrain, Saudi Arabia, Jordan, and Morocco.[6] The US tilted towards short-term security and away from nurturing lasting political change in the name of long-term security.[7] The Trump administration moved further in this direction, as it focused support on "our friends", even where these were autocracies. Trump sought to cooperate with autocrats like Kim Jong-un and professed affinity for authoritarian leaders around the globe, such as Vladimir Putin.[8]

European democracy support also plateaued. While the EU continued to produce democracy strategies, its core foreign policy document of the decade, a Global Strategy released in 2016, was widely seen as far more realpolitik in tone than previous such templates. In the 2010s, it became progressively more circumspect in its use of political conditionality – that is, in its linking of aid and trade offers to human rights and democracy improvements. The democracy clause in its external agreements was not invoked outside

---

[6] Ibid.
[7] Robert Pee, "Obama has put national security ahead of promoting democracy abroad", *The Conversation*, August 10, 2016, https://theconversation.com/obama-has-put-national-security-ahead-of-promoting-democracy-abroad-62711.
[8] Council on Foreign Relations, Candidate Tracker: Donald J. Trump, 2020, https://www.cfr.org/election2020/candidate-tracker/donald-j.-trump.

of sub-Saharan Africa. The EU has declined to remove GSP trade preferences from countries like Pakistan and the Philippines, where human rights have clearly worsened. While the EU offered support to the Arab Spring revolts that began in 2001, it then adopted a hands-off approach as Middle Eastern and North African governments pushed back against democracy. Some of the biggest increases in European aid went to authoritarian regimes, especially under a new trust fund structure set up to quell the surge in migrant flows in 2016. The democratic elements of EU peacebuilding and stabilization missions dwindled. European positions towards China softened during the decade.[9]

Non-Western Democracies: Rising but Cautious

Many non-Western rising powers that prospered strongly in the 2010s were democracies, and they showed some increased interest in shoring up democratic values internationally as they become more significant foreign-policy actors. However, they remained cautious about de-

---

[9] R. Youngs (2021). *The European Union and Global Politics*, Macmillan, chapter 9.

veloping strong or systematic commitments to democracy internationally.

There were certainly examples of these rising democracies contributing to global democratic dynamics. Brazil took on a leading role in Haiti's political and economic reconstruction, while pushing for Latin American regional bodies such as Mercosur and the Organization of American States to adopt strong democracy protection clauses. Argentina, Brazil, and Chile reacted strongly to a 2009 military coup in Honduras and responded to a quite different type of coup against Paraguay's sitting president in 2012. At these same states' behest, the Organization of American States introduced an Inter-American Democracy Charter, and most other Latin American collective organizations introduced democracy clauses aimed at defending incumbent regimes from coup attempts.

Indonesia pushed hard for the Association of Southeast Asian Nations (ASEAN) to incorporate into the group's 2008 charter several dialogue forums on democracy support and a commitment to defending democratic norms. The country oriented itself as a leading diplomatic advocate for political reforms in Myanmar and, to some extent, in Cambodia and Vietnam as well. India played a major role in helping the Nepalese government and Maoist insurgents reach a democratic peace deal in 2006. It also developed many pro-democracy initiatives and diplomatic efforts in Sri Lanka. Turkey initially positioned itself as perhaps the most engaged external player in the Arab Spring uprisings of 2011 and committed itself to supporting democratic change in the region. South Africa pushed for a democratic resolution to a 2011 electoral crisis in Côte d'Ivoire and sought to build democracy concerns into regional conflict prevention initiatives.

Many of these non-Western democracies invested money in democracy support and established aid programs that included meaningful amounts of financial backing for political reform initiatives. Indonesia began funding so-called South-South cooperation on democratic governance after 2010. The country's Institute for Peace and Democracy ran a wide range of democracy assistance initiatives in Myanmar and other ASEAN countries, gradually moving into more sensitive areas such as security sector reform. Japan rolled out a widening portfolio of aid projects covering election assistance, police reforms, and the rule of law – efforts that amounted to a few hundred million dollars per year by the late 2000s. Similarly, Turkey's sizable aid budget included an array of funding for judicial reforms, civil society, security-sector reforms, and institution building. South Africa funded election observers in many other African countries.

Geopolitical factors were often behind these non-Western strategies. In Asia, leading countries like Japan and India saw democracy support as a means of pushing back against China's rise. For large emerging countries like Brazil and Indonesia, advocacy for democratic causes offered a way to reinforce their claims to regional leadership. And for other actors, like Turkey's ruling party, the Justice and Development Party (AKP), democracy promotion was a means of backing close ideological affiliates in other countries.

However, in general these rising or non-Western democracies were hesitant in their defence of democratic norms. Their policies remained relatively modest and, in many cases, became less values-based and more realpolitik as the decade unfolded. In Africa, the African Charter for Democracy, Elections, and Governance seemed to run out of steam and did little to counter the continent's authoritarian turn. In Latin America, support for democracy got caught up in the region's fraught division between leftist and right-wing governments; left-leaning democratic governments declined to invoke any democratic clauses or instruments against democratic backsliding observed in Venezuela and Nicaragua. Brazil, India, and South Africa held back from supporting democracy more strongly due to their desire to craft an interlocking set of partnerships with Russia and China under the BRICS banner. The more democratic India-Brazil-South Africa (IPSA) Dialogue Forum issued many statements stressing support for democracy and human rights but faded in importance.

Moreover, there was limited coordination among democracies. Proposals for a concert or league of democracies were raised and circulated briefly in the mid-2000s. But neither Western nor non-Western governments pursued these ideas with any conviction, and such thinking soon subsided. European governments were (justifiably) unenthusiastic, fearing that such groupings would undermine the United Nations. The Community of Democracies (CoD) was created in 2000, expanded to 106 members, and ran many projects and dialogue forums. However, it fell short of its initial ambitions and lost momentum. The CoD included many nondemocratic states, complicating its utility as an operational democracy support body and making it more akin to a venue for inclusive dialogue. While the CoD runs useful low-level initiatives, it has neither gained high-level strategic traction nor practical operational democracy support initiatives on the ground.

Renewed Commitment?

Against this backdrop, democratic states have slowly begun to respond to the geopolitical threats to liberal values. Since the early 2020s, deepening geopolitical tension has in at least some measure become a spur to stronger commitments to defend democratic values.

The COVID-19 pandemic served as a wake-up call. China's provision of vaccines around the world and its assertive COVID-19-related diplomacy added a further dimension to sharpened geopolitical rivalries across the world. Some democracies' clear mismanagement of the crisis left a dent in global dynamics supportive of democratic norms. The fact that China provided far more vaccines to developing states than Western countries did little for democracy's global appeal. Western governments' refusal to allow in those with Chinese vaccinations damaged the image of the democratic world in the eyes of many citizens around the world.

But this situation was by now so serious that it appeared to prompt democracies into some degree of action. Some noted that democracies have finally come to see China as a systemic and belligerent enough threat to band together to defend the liberal order and democracy. Some diplomats now saw democracy support as more of a strategic priority. Increasingly, democratic nations have come to worry that China threatens democracy everywhere, including in their own countries.

Nearly all democracies have begun to wean themselves off of such a high dependency on Chinese exports. All of them are introducing barriers to outside interference in democratic processes as a response to both Chinese and Russian tactics of incursion. The democratic nations have begun to explore hard security coordination too, reflecting a concern to defend democracy in the most immediate way. In Asia, the Quad, made up of four democratic nations, has become more active and framed its mission more expressly in terms of democracy needing to counter authoritarianism.

The Biden administration has shown a stronger commitment to democracy than US governments have for many years. It moved quickly to impose democracy-related sanctions on a range of countries, including Belarus, Bosnia and Herzegovina, Burma, China, Cuba, Ecuador,

Honduras, Kenya, Nicaragua, North Macedonia, Russia, Somalia, and Sudan. It issued a new Strategy to Prevent Conflict and Promote Stability that defines priorities democracy as its clear foreign policy priority. The Administration's budget requests have aimed to expand funding for democracy, human rights protection, good governance promotion, anti-corruption efforts, and gender equality. Early 2022 saw the first time that a US administration refrained from using a national security waiver to give aid despite a lack of compliance with human rights conditions: The State Department decided to permanently withhold $130 million in security assistance to Egypt.

Similar changes were forthcoming in European democracy support. The EU strengthened its commitments under a new Democracy and Human Rights Action Plan for 2020–2020. The union launched its new Global Human Rights Sanctions Regime and increased other sanctions to a record level, including in Belarus, Myanmar, Russia and Venezuela. European aid was cut or reduced for these and other democratic backsliders like Afghanistan, Ethiopia, Mali and Turkey. The EU increased democracy funding under its 2020–2027 budget and made its funding rules more agile and flexible; 1.5 billion euros were allocated for democracy and human rights and another 1.5 billion euros for civil society in third countries, while the Commission promised 15 percent, or 9 billion euros, of geographical aid would also go to democracy-related aims.

In 2021 a new Team Europe Democracy initiative got member states to contribute to joint democracy programmes and efforts around the world, coordinated by a new German-managed secretariat. New EU strategies for the Indo-Pacific, Africa and the Mena region all promised more support for democratic reformers, while a Global Gateway initiative promised mixed public-private funds that would be an alternative to China's Belt and Road Initiative and a way of funding infrastructure compatible with democratic values. A handful of European governments introduced their own national democracy strategies separate from these EU-level initiatives and increased funding under them.[10]

Japan has upgraded its discursive commitment to defending democratic values in the last several years. It has done so through policy initiatives like the Free and Open Indo-Pacific concept, its bilateral security agreements with other democracies such as India and Australia, and multilateral agreements with other democra-

---

[10] European Democracy Hub, European Democracy Support Annual Review 2021.

cies such as the Japan-EU Economic Partnership Agreement. Its foreign aid has focused more on good governance and some rights issues. South Korea has followed suit. It has increased its contributions to the UN Democracy Fund. The Korean foreign aid agency has increased funding for good governance in developing countries. South Korea has also developed the Association of World Election Bodies to assist elections in developing countries. The country also took an unprecedented step by imposing government sanctions against the Myanmar military after the military coup in 2021. Korea is getting more active, with projects in the last couple of years beyond the immediate region in places like Bangladesh, Gambia, Kenya and Senegal. Some donors are moving away from projects towards core support.

In India, Prime Minister Modi's government has pursued a foreign policy that preferentially engages or supports fellow democracies. Modi strongly and routinely emphasizes India's democracy as the key to its global identity. He stresses the democratic elements of India's economic assistance abroad, for example, in opening Mauritius' new Supreme Court building, which was supported by Indian funding. India has revived its financial support for the UN Democracy Fund and participation in Community of Democracies ministerial meetings. It uses increasingly clear pro-democracy language in joint diplomatic statements such as the Quad or the EU-India summit. India has channelled increasing amounts of overseas aid through its Development Partnership Administration, which was created in 2012. Through a unit of its electoral commission focused specifically on external support, India has deployed sizable teams and significant resources to train electoral officials and monitor elections in countries like Libya, Namibia, and South Africa. Latin American democracies have finally sought to mobilise regional clauses and policy tools against authoritarianism in Venezuela and Nicaragua as well as right-wing authoritarian populism in El Salvador and elsewhere.

The Summit for Democracy

A potentially key point in these incipient democratic geopolitics came with the commitment of the new Biden administration to hold a Summit for Democracy in order to kickstart a process of strategic coordination between democratic governments around the world. A virtual summit was held in December 2021. The arrangements were complicated by the US's decisions over who to invite and not invite. After much debate, the Biden administration invited 110 leaders. While these represented governments that were democratic in some kind or degree, the US excluded some states such as Bolivia, Bosnia, Gambia, Hungary, Lebanon and Sri Lanka that had a higher democracy score than many of those that were invited. While the summit was broadly a democratic gathering, political interests and rivalries were not entirely absent from the arrangements.

Democracies around the world participated in the summit, although with some misgivings. South Korea and Japan participated, even though they were concerned about the US using the summit as an anti-China alliance. Japan did not want the summit to be an exclusive democracy grouping, mainly for fear that the US would exclude some Southeast Asian countries of strategic importance to Japan. The Indian government engaged with the summit process, even though the fact that the summit was being hosted by the United States to some degree lessened its enthusiasm. India was increasingly keen to use the democracy narrative principally to demarcate India strategically from China and present an alternative model of governance to other developing democracies – and it saw the summit through this lens.

The US and other Western states stated a commitment to being open to non-Western powers' concerns and ideas in order to get them to participate fully. Still, non-Western democracies expressed concerns about the process being seen as a process led heavy-handedly by Western, developed countries in accordance with their own democratic templates. They were not keen on a formal charter, a large secretariat, formal entry criteria, rigid rules of participation, and the like. They were all uneasy about a process of democratic coordination being moulded around the US's judgements of other states' democratic credentials and its own geostrategic interests. While broadly positive towards international cooperation on democracy, they did not want to be associated with any new democratic interventionism. Some Asian invitees, like Malaysia, Mongolia and Pakistan, did not attend, allegedly for fear of stirring Chinese resentment. Asian democracies were cautious in addressing abuses inside China but were more supportive at the summit of mobilizing a common democratic community against China's coercive tactics outside its borders.

The 2021 summit established a wider process of democratic coordination, leading up to a second summit set for March 2023. After the summit, the attending governments made commitments to strengthen democracy at home, and around a third promised to upgrade their international democracy support. Most of the commitments were fairly general and non-specific, but some were notably concrete. It was difficult to separate out which reforms were already in the pipeline and which were entirely new as a result of the summit *per se*. US commitments to strengthen democracy abroad were far ahead of any others, as it promised to upgrade a range of existing anti-corruption programmes, add funds to the Embattled CSOs Assistance Fund and create a new post for democratic renewal abroad. Even if it was difficult to isolate the impact of the new summit process itself, as old internal and external commitments mixed with new initiatives, it clearly gave something of a fillip to international democratic coordination.[11]

The Russian Invasion and Beyond

The Russian invasion of Ukraine is an inflection point that may push democratic coordination further in this direction. In the wake of the invasion, President Biden declared that "We are engaged anew in a great battle for freedom. A battle between democracy and autocracy. Between

---
[11] International IDEA.

liberty and repression". Prominent analysts talk of a reinvigorated commitment to defending the liberal order and democratic norms. They argue that the battle for Ukraine is part of a broader battle for democracy and against autocratic and illiberal values. The war has already unleashed a far stronger determination to defend the liberal order.

For now, the democracy-autocracy divide is not absolutely predominant. India and South Africa abstained from the United Nations resolution on the invasion. Democratic Israel refused to sanction Russia, while authoritarian Singapore adopted sanctions. The group of 141 states that voted to condemn Russia at the United Nations included many non-democracies. Not all democracies lined up against Russia, and not all autocracies lined up behind it.

Both the EU and the US are seeking deeper cooperation with authoritarian regimes to help counter Russia. European states are reaching out to Gulf suppliers to replace Russian gas, and the US is even turning to Venezuela for oil supplies. Western democracies have been seeking support from authoritarian states and pressing them into action against Russia.

There is certainly more coordination among Western democracies to protect themselves from

Russian aggression. For the moment, it is not certain that this will also entail stronger support for democracy globally. The invasion has certainly awoken new rhetorical commitment in this sense. If this sentiment is translated into concrete pro-democratic coordination, and if this can include democracies from all regions, then this could be a significant turning point in international democracy support. For now, the risk remains that realpolitik and differences between democracies could cancel out this potential.

About the Author

Richard Youngs is a senior fellow in the Democracy, Conflict and Governance programme at the Carnegie Endowment for International Peace, and professor of international relations at the University of Warwick. He is co-founder and co-director of the European Democracy Hub.

A Conflict Resolution Perspective on Democracy Promotion

Lukas Probst Lopez

Since the end of the Cold War, we have witnessed a reconfiguration of the balance of power in the world. While the transition from the brief unipolar moment following 1989 to a multipolar world order was never likely to be smooth, it has, in the last few years, accelerated and led to both a global increase in conflicts[1] and a democratic recession.[2]

As geopolitical rivalry intensifies in the wake of the war against Ukraine, the world is increasingly being viewed as divided into a "democratic" and an "authoritarian" camp. Consequently, political mobilization to shore up democracy is growing. There is a growing realization that in an increasingly insecure world, democracy can no longer be taken for granted and that democratic institutions need to be pro-

---

[1] Conflict Trends: A Global Overview, 1946–2021, https://www.prio.org/publications/13178.
[2] https://v-dem.net/documents/29/V-dem_democracyreport2023_lowres.pdf.

tected both from external attacks and internal erosion. Policymakers and the broader public alike mull issues such as dwindling civic participation, the fallout of rapid digitalization and polarization through social media (see the chapter by Idayat Hassan in this volume) and how best to defend the integrity of democratic processes from foreign meddling. Furthermore, global challenges such as the COVID pandemic or the climate crisis require democracies to navigate the fine balance between the imperative of social solidarity and the protection of fundamental freedoms. Unlike autocracies, democracies always face the dilemma that measures implemented in the name of upholding democracy (e.g. restrictions on freedom of speech) may be abused to strengthen the government's grip on power. This can, in turn, enhance cleavages in society and boost those very forces that are supposed to be anti-democratic.

A Resurgence in Democracy Promotion?

Democracies are not only looking inward to strengthen their resilience in the face of adversity. At the same time, there is also a resurgence in democracy promotion abroad with a view to expanding and strengthening the "democratic camp" in the world. The main focus lies on countries ranging somewhere on the spectrum between autocracies, hybrid regimes, and semi-consolidated democracies.[3] For the most part, these countries are very much on the fence between the two camps, as many stand much to lose from increased competition and confrontation between geopolitical blocs. Furthermore, many of these countries are poor to middle-income states and are often afflicted by conflicts that intersect in multiple ways with the way that state power is wielded. A number of them also fall into the category of highly fragile states, where high levels of poverty are compounded by at least one or several forms of violence and conflict.

As Richard Youngs' paper points out, it remains to be seen to what extent the rhetoric will be followed by concrete action for democracy support worldwide, but both the USA and the EU seem bullish, launching political initiatives such as the Summit for Democracy and channeling increased funding towards democracy promotion and the protection of human rights. Switzerland, too, will increase its focus on democracy promotion in the framework of its upcoming Foreign

---

[3] https://freedomhouse.org/sites/default/files/2022-04/NIT_2022_final_digital.pdf.

Policy and International Cooperation Strategies.[4] Conversely, there is no such political momentum and drive for increased funding discernible with regard to conflict resolution and peacebuilding work. It is nothing new that diplomacy and the peaceful resolution of conflict are characterized as futile endeavors in times of war, but that there simultaneously seems to be a renewed impetus to promote and support democracy should give us pause for thought.

After all, do conflict resolution and democracy promotion not share the same goals and challenges? This article argues that rooting democracy promotion in conflict resolution provides many practical benefits. Firstly, it helps to overcome the clash between different norms that have trapped democracy promotion in the past. Secondly, it allows for an understanding of conflict resolution not merely as a practical tool for

---

[4] In International Cooperation, Swiss Development Cooperation (SDC) has focused on what it used to call "governance" for over 20 years, supporting democratic practices, strengthening accountability of state institutions, building the capacity of civil society, supporting independent media, local governance and political, financial and administrative decentralization. The stronger focus on democracy means that it strengthens its work on anti-corruption cooperation and retains its focus also on democracy promotion in a narrower sense (parliament and electoral support).

resolving individual conflicts but as a "political system" in its own right.[5]

Two Distinct but Interrelated Endeavors

While conflict resolution and democracy promotion have many similarities and, following Kant's famous treatise on perpetual peace, arguably aim towards the same *outcome*, there are also a few important differences, in particular at the level of *process*. As regards the former, this short article can't do justice to the rich literature on democratic peace that has developed since Kant's time. Nor can it adequately summarize and analyze the diverse practices in democracy promotion and conflict resolution that have emerged since the end of World War II. I will therefore limit myself to a brief overview here.

In general, the discussion on the interrelation between peace and democracy is subdivided into two main strands: Democratic states' ability to deal with conflicts *internally* and, secondly, democratic states' ability to uphold *peaceful re-*

---

[5] J. W. Burton (1988). *Conflict Resolution as a Political System*, ICAR Working Paper No. 1, http://mars.gmu.edu/bitstream/handle/1920/10674/SCAR_WP_1.pdf?sequence=1&isAllowed=y.

lationships with other states.⁶ The latter is generally further subdivided into a monadic theory (democratic states fight fewer wars than autocracies) and a dyadic theory (democracies fight fewer wars against other democracies). Evidence that democracies rarely fight wars against other democracies is well substantiated, while the evidence that democracies fight fewer wars in general is much more circumstantial. The argument that democracies are particularly well suited to promote and uphold peace internally is also debated. In many countries, the transition towards democracy is also accompanied by increased conflict.⁷ Examples of attempted transitions that have failed and led to increased conflict can be found all over the world, from Southeast Asia to Africa, and of course, the revolutions that started out as the "Arab Spring". The democratic peace paradigm has therefore come under increased scrutiny, both for its alleged normative bias towards Western secular culture and for its patchy record in countries transitioning from armed conflict to peace.⁸ Nevertheless, the *cor-*

---

[6] See, for example, O. Ramsbotham, T. Woodhouse, H. Miall (2016): *Contemporary Conflict Resolution, Fourth Edition* (Cambridge: Polity Press), 331-333.

[7] E. Mansfield and J. Snyder (2005). *Electing to fight: Why emerging democracies go to war* (Cambridge: MIT Press.

[8] See, for example: https://www.accord.org.za/conflict-trends/challenges-liberal-peace-statebuilding-divid

relation between peace and democracy is widely acknowledged, while the *causality* is a matter of much debate, and many "developmental autocracies" argue that peace and development come first, while respect for human rights and democracy must be deferred.

Despite the fact that there is a broad and varied literature on democratic peace and that concrete efforts to promote democracy and resolve conflict in fragile states are often undertaken by the same set of actors (the United Nations, various international NGOs and state actors engaging in development cooperation, and peace-, state- and nation-building), the relation between democracy promotion and conflict resolution remains somewhat strained. This mostly has to do with a certain malaise with the term of democracy promotion.

As Simon Geissbühler's paper points out, democracy promotion has fallen into disrepute chiefly due to a number of (military) interventions, which, regardless of their purported successes in other areas, have definitively put to rest the idea that democracy can be im-

---

ed-societies. For a thoughtful "critique of the critiques" of liberal peacebuilding see: R. Paris: "Saving liberal peacebuilding" in *Review of International Studies* (2010), 337-365.

posed from the outside. This has understandably led many scholars and practitioners of conflict resolution to give short shrift to the concept of democracy promotion, often seen as forcefully pushing a Western-centric agenda and insensitive to local realities and pre-existing institutions. The conflict resolution field tends to be wary of approaches that propose "outside solutions", championing participation, local ownership and bringing actors (conflict parties) around the table to develop their own solutions. Even if the means used are peaceful and well-intentioned, an approach as unabashedly normative as democracy promotion is not easily reconciled with the basic principles of conflict resolution. Nevertheless, it must also be acknowledged that there is an inherent tension in the field of conflict resolution between its universalist claims refuting any one normative grounding and the fact that it (knowingly or unknowingly) tends to reproduce (Western) democratic models. Bochsler and Juon's paper's insights into the role of mediators and their personal experience of power-sharing arrangements seem to confirm as much and rightly call for further research into these dynamics.

Therefore, as international democracy promotion looks set to ramp up and much of this effort will likely be directed at fragile and conflict-affected states, it may be a good moment to briefly reflect on what we need to take into account so that the promotion of democracy does not end up fomenting new conflicts and delivers on the promise of democracy as a form of rule "of the people, by the people and for the people".

Towards the Next Generation of Democracy Promotion?

Firstly, we need to acknowledge the changing environment in which both conflict resolution and democracy promotion take place. Even if the risk of a renewed Cold War becomes ever greater and we are seemingly returning to a new form of a bipolar world order, the division of the world into an autocratic and a democratic camp seems overly simplistic and does not do justice to the fact that the balance of economic and political power in the world has shifted considerably. It follows that many countries will not choose a clear alignment with one or the other camp. The recent voting patterns at the United Nations provide a useful illustration of this fractured state of affairs.[9] This has conse-

---

[9] https://foreignpolicy.com/2023/03/08/russia-ukraine-war-west-global-south-diplomacy-un-putin-g20/.

quences for democracy promotion as well, as it opens up space for multiple points of reference along which countries may choose to orient themselves. While some countries may agree with democratic decision-making, they may at the same time disapprove of the social liberalism associated with the traditional Western model of democracy. Therefore, it is important that democracy promotion be a truly universal effort and not the purview of a few Western countries. Furthermore, countries that have undergone democratic transitions more recently than many Western countries are often better placed to understand the political and societal tensions that democratization brings with it.

Secondly, the next generation of democracy promotion will take place in a context where a certain measure of erosion can increasingly be witnessed also in consolidated democracies. While this provides a compelling reason to reinvigorate democracy worldwide, it also bears the risk that democracy promotion follows a "threat and response logic", where democracies "defend" themselves against authoritarian regimes. The development of a stronger narrative that puts the many advantages of democratic governance back into the center of international discourse is a necessary and welcome development. However, promoting democracy abroad should not be forcibly pursued or come with strings attached. Needless to say, this would also greatly compromise efforts to resolve conflict, which aim to accommodate diverging interests, foster compromise between hardline positions and ultimately broker mutually acceptable solutions between conflict parties. Like conflict resolution, the development of democratic institutions is (or should be) largely an endemic, locally owned endeavor. Admittedly, this is a long and arduous process that requires much patience and will likely also experience setbacks. It is, however, necessary given the long list of procedural and illiberal democracies that respect the form but not the substance of democracy and deliver little in the way of peace and development to the population.

Thirdly, democracy promotion has for too long focused mostly on elections with, as we now know, demonstrably mixed results in fragile and conflict-elected contexts. On the one hand, democratically held elections constitute a fitting ending to a peace process and serve as an important moment for the population to move on from a difficult past and lay the groundwork for the future. As such, elections can lend broader legitimacy to peace agreements that are oftentimes the product of elite bargaining. On the other hand, elections are also a stress test of the highest order for a fractured and conflict-affected polity that, at times, must integrate armed actors turned political parties. Taking the crucial step from enemy (on the battlefield) to political opponent is often difficult. Admittedly, the United Nations and other international actors have made great progress and increasingly integrate a conflict prevention perspective into their support for electoral processes, which all too often were handled in a mostly procedural, logistical and "technical" manner. Nevertheless, the strong international insistence on "free and fair" elections with a "one (wo)man, one vote approach" is often perceived by local actors as a push for regime change, leading to pushback and directing all political attention towards elections. The more fundamental point here is that the question of democratic legitimacy cannot be reduced to elections, which are a competitive and therefore particularly conflictual element of democracy. In some countries, the population would rather give a mandate to their group than any one single person, which is antithetical to the general understanding of democracy in the Western tradition. From a conflict prevention perspective, it is therefore crucial to give equal support to other aspects that strengthen the legitimacy of politics: Capacity building for political parties and parliaments, support for independent media and civil society are just some examples. Needless to say, these too are long-term endeavors that may come too late if initiated just before elections or even over the duration of an electoral cycle.

Fourthly, many newer efforts to promote democracy abroad do in fact respect many conflict resolution principles, prioritizing local ownership and participatory processes and basing their interventions on thorough conflict analyses and do no harm principles. Nevertheless, much of the work that is done is based on identifying, adapting and implementing democratic models and institutional arrangements that have been developed elsewhere. While many of these efforts do lead to tangible results, they remain, no matter how sensitive to contextual specificities, prone to reifying highly complex sociopolitical dynamics, and therefore often not sustainable. Mark Warren suggests a problem-based and pragmatic approach to democratic theory that may be more promising: *"What kinds of problems does a political system need to solve to count as "democratic"?"*[10] This is very much consistent with conflict resolution, which puts joint problem-solving at the heart of many of its interventions. It also helps to avoid normative "dead-

---

[10] M. Warren (2017). "A Problem-Based Approach to Democratic Theory" *American Political Science Review*, 39-53.

ends" and allows for the development of various democratic practices reflecting the polarized world we live in. Problem-solving approaches have also been adopted in the areas of governance and public sector reform, including in the OECD.[11] The lessons learned there would also seem to apply to democracy promotion.

Conclusion

Kant and many after him have envisaged a cosmopolitan order of democracy with some form of "world government" that would achieve "perpetual peace". Clearly, this vision seems far out of reach in today's world. This article has mainly argued that overly normative approaches towards democracy promotion are likely to fail in the current fractured world order. Viewing democracy (promotion) primarily as a way of solving concrete conflicts not only in developing countries but increasingly also in consolidated democracies may provide a pragmatic way forward. I have been less explicit about the lessons for the field of conflict resolution, which must also become more cognizant of some of its nor-

---

[11] A. Christie et al.: "Quick Guide to Development Co-operation Innovation for Public Sector Reform" https://www.oecd.org/dac/accountable-effective-institutions/DAC%20Innovation%20Guide%20v22.pdf.

mative biases that underlie "liberal peacemaking". Also, the field is at risk of losing sight of some of its foundational principles, such as impartiality (towards conflict parties), sustainability (of interventions) and consistency (across different theatres of conflict). We are currently witnessing an increase in high-powered diplomacy and short-term deal-making that prioritizes security at the expense of underlying societal issues that lead to conflict. While such deals, which generally involve many hard-won compromises, may be a necessary element to end violence, they will not lead to long-term sustainable peace without popular support. If we lose sight of democracy and the necessary popular support for such deals, we may also risk losing the art of conflict resolution.

About the Author

Lukas Probst Lopez is a career diplomat with a background in conflict transformation and peacebuilding. He joined the Federal Department of Foreign Affairs in 2010 and currently heads the Mediation Section in the Peace and Human Rights Division. He earned an M.A. in International Relations from the Graduate Institute of International and Development Studies in Geneva.

Current Democratic Challenges and Opportunities

Elections as a Pathway to Democracy – Challenges in Practice for the Diplomatic Community

Hannah ROBERTS

Upping our game on elections is more important than ever given the current context of democratic backsliding. If we are to go beyond democracy narratives, we need to consider how, in practice, we can promote elections that meet citizens' and societies' immediate and long-term interests. We now have decades of practice from which we can learn. This paper seeks to critically reflect on the challenges involved in elections and the diplomatic community's promotion of credible, transparent, and inclusive processes.

Introduction

The global decline in democracy includes a deterioration in electoral processes. For example, the V-dem 2022 report notes that, in the context of the "wiping out" of advances in global levels of democracy made over the last 35 years, the quality of elections is worsening in 30 countries.[1] This decline is affecting a range of countries, showing that electoral processes are subject to change, positive and negative, and need ongoing monitoring and protection. The deterioration raises questions about how electoral practices can be developed in different contexts, and what role the international community can play (including what actions to avoid and how we can best be effective).

Elections are obviously critical, as they are an integral part of the democratic architecture. Therefore, if we want to promote democracy, we need to deal with elections in some way or another. They are a huge opportunity to promote participation, accountability, and agreement on dealing with problems and ways forward. They are crucial to the alternation of power and, therefore, to mitigating the risk of entrenchment, state capture, and autocracy. They are perhaps the most visible manifestation of democratic functioning.

However, elections are necessary but not sufficient. They are one part of a democratic ecosystem but have sometimes been overly focused

---

[1] Democracy Report 2023 – Defiance in the Face of Autocratization, V-Dem Institute, 2023.

on by the international community. There has at times been an international need to hold good elections to show that democracy is triumphing and becoming established, with attention then quickly turning to other matters. For example, elections in Afghanistan in 2004 and 2005 were a narrow and fragile gain that were just a starting point, not an end in themselves.

It may also be argued that we have **overemphasized elected representatives and have undervalued other deliberative democracy mechanisms**. For example, citizen assemblies, which enable a cross-section of the public to become expertly informed and make policy recommendations, have the advantage that recommendations are more likely to be based on long-term societal benefit rather than short-term electoral and party interests. However, there remains a need for elections, with parties bringing continuity and accountability.

Intrinsic Challenges with Elections

While elections bring great opportunity, they also have various risks that need to be guarded against to avoid perilous forms of democracy. Without such guarding, elections may be held, but they will not serve their purpose of enabling effective democratic government based on the will of the people. Without such guarding, there is a risk that, rather than helping societies survive and thrive, elections undermine democratic functioning and confidence.

One inherent risk is that elections become a system for mob rule, whereby those with numerical strength can make decisions in their own interests rather than for the greater or long-term good. This can be summed up in a phrase attributed to Benjamin Franklin but apparently not said by him. It states, "Democracy is two wolves and a lamb voting on what to have for lunch. Liberty is a well-armed lamb contesting the vote". There is therefore a need to be "well-armed" and to have rule-of-law and human rights safeguards to protect against mob rule through elections.

A second intrinsic risk is that elections become a mere popularity contest, rather than being about substance and working out solutions to problems and ways forward. This populist approach deprioritises the resolution of issues and promotes crowd-pleasing actions without consideration for long-term interests. Frameworks are needed that pivot parties and voters to substantive matters, including factual realities and societal challenges, not just candidate narratives.

A third intrinsic risk is that elections become a system for power entrenchment with a democratic façade. The V-dem 2022 report classifies 56 countries as "electoral autocracies". This can be especially pronounced when the checks in a political system and electoral process are weak and when citizens are not in a position to make their own free choices. A genuine election process involves many legal, political, and technical factors that need to be worked out according to the unique circumstances of a country and evolving electoral dynamics.

A fourth intrinsic risk is that elections become divisive and a trigger for violence and instability. Competition can become dangerous, especially when there are high stakes, elevated levels of societal frustration and division, and low levels of confidence in the electoral process and access to remedies. Violence is at times employed strategically to manipulate an electoral process and increase bargaining clout. Elections need to be free from violence, have integrity, and be genuine if they are to contribute to long-term peaceful democratic development. Warning signs of dangerous divisions and violence can typically be seen well ahead of an election and some mitigations can be made. For example, by promoting the responsibilities of leaders, dialogue and engagement between contenders, as well as with authorities, the election administration is seen to be transparent and fair, with meaningful opportunities for remedy through appeals processes.

Other More Contemporary Challenges

Additionally, there are contemporary challenges, not least regarding the digital and information revolutions taking place at this time. Technology and social media bring new possibilities for efficiency, transparency, reliability, and communication, but also new risks. We've seen how difficult it is for election administrations, which can be under intense political pressure, to use technology in practice and to provide for stakeholder confidence. Private international companies are now involved in the critical infrastructure of elections, often with limited oversight and protections. We've seen how untransparent social media advertising and messaging is, with insufficient accounting of who is sending what. We've seen the lack of protection for citizens' privacy and data, which can be used to the advantage of powerful interests. We've seen disinformation sow confusion and undermine good decision-making. All of these can distort people's ability to deliberate and think freely, and ultimately to make their own choices. Globally, we are struggling to keep up with the changes and establish legal limitations, oversight mechanisms, and practical actions that safeguard voters, candidates, and the electoral process.

In this environment, powerful, problematic election narratives can thrive and disrupt political order. Corrupt narratives can dominate population groups, for example, by asserting forcefully that elections have been stolen without necessarily relating to reality and sometimes despite black-and-white evidence to the contrary. These can trigger instability and violence, especially with rapid communication and polluted information environments. The narratives of an election matter as much as the numbers. Thus, there is a need for strong transparency and data provision from multiple agencies and organisations, clear information and messaging from a range of actors, and robust independent scrutiny.

Another contemporary challenge comes from increasingly sophisticated and subtle attempts at electoral corruption and interference. Corruption can be facilitated by laws or administrative actions that enable unchecked decision-making, obfuscation, and opportunity for selective advantage, thereby undermining an election process. Manipulations can, of course, come from contenders, for example, by misusing the resources of incumbency or seeking to intimidate voters or election officials. Interference can also come from external actors seeking to influence voters and the system without transparency (such as is alleged in regard to Russia and the US elections and Brexit). Corporate bodies may also use financial heft to promote commercial or political interests. While seeking influence may be seen as legitimate, when done through untransparent means, it becomes interference. Therefore, a range of robust regulations, transparency measures, and enforcement mechanisms are needed that evolve with emerging challenges.

A further contemporary challenge is democratic disillusionment and disengagement, resulting in low levels of participation and consequent legitimacy. With low voter turnout, those elected become less accountable, thus risking poorer decision-making. International IDEA has noted that "Voter turnout has been declining across the globe since the beginning of 1990s".[2] The recent 2023 Nigerian elections may be seen as an example of this, with a turnout of only approximately 27% for the presidential election. It

---

[2] Voter Turnout Trends Around the World, International IDEA 2016. Also International IDEA's Global State of Democracy Report 2021 notes that voter turnout in most countries dropped during the pandemic.

can be hard for people to vote when elections are seen as a rotation (if you're lucky) of corruption. People may also choose not to engage or vote if elections seem violent and/or fuel intolerance, or if they don't trust the electoral process to be fair. Therefore, in addition to having a range of convincing contenders, it's critical to have strong electoral processes with checks and balances to promote confidence in participating.

These difficulties can be critical, as without good elections, we risk losing democratic dividends and benefits. People will find other ways for their voices to be heard, for example, by going to the streets, with risks of instability and possible violence. Therefore, the international community needs to engage with the ongoing challenge of promoting positive election processes. This is not about the outcome of an election but about the *process* being democratically effective.

Difficulties in Promoting Good Elections

However, it can be challenging to promote good election processes, not least because they are seen as a very sovereign matter. While this is true, electoral rights are also an integral part of human rights and, therefore, fall under established multilateral instruments and systems. These instruments have near universal applicability and, therefore, authority. For example, the International Covenant on Civil and Political Rights (ICCPR) has 173 countries that are parties to the treaty.[3] The treaty states that:

Every citizen shall have the right and the opportunity, without any of the distinctions mentioned in article 2 and without unreasonable restrictions: (a) To take part in the conduct of public affairs, directly or through freely chosen representatives; (b) To vote and to be elected at genuine periodic elections which shall be by universal and equal suffrage and shall be held by secret ballot, guaranteeing the free expression of the will of the electors.[4]

Other key ICCPR obligations relevant to electoral processes include the right to remedy, freedom from discrimination, and the fundamental freedoms of assembly, association, expression, and movement. Thus, these instruments provide key guardrails for an election process. There are also comparable commitments in regional treaties, for example in the African Union's Charter on Democracy, Elections and Governance. Therefore, when we look at elections and

---

[3] ICCPR ratification status, UN Treaty Body Database.
[4] ICCPR, article 25.

support electoral processes in other countries, we can refer to the standards a country has itself chosen through signing up to international treaties and political agreements.

Another challenge in promoting good elections is that electoral matters are complex, involving many interrelated political and technical factors. It is often hard to follow what is going on, with limited information, confusing technicalities, and subtler forms of distortion. It can sometimes be hard to know what is deliberate corruption and what is an unintended mess, though usually the two feed off each other. Electoral processes can therefore be hard to perfectly predict, and it can be difficult to measure the impact of any support. It is the job of observers, both citizens and international, to go into these complexities. Increasingly, other forms of scrutiny are also needed, for example, from academics and investigative journalists with different roles and mandates who can often go deeper and cover longer time periods.

A further challenge with promoting election reform is that there can be strong countervailing vested political interests. Addressing issues on a purely technical basis can risk missing bigger picture problems with an election, with technical assistance potentially inadvertently reinforcing a sham or quasi-election. Thus, evolving political dynamics need to be continuously assessed and considered when we look at how we support good election processes. There can often be a lack of political will for electoral reform and a conflict of interest, with those in power typically not wanting to change the system that brought them in. Thus, diplomatic political engagement is needed, as is development and cooperation support. Such engagement can cost some political capital but can also be positive in demonstrating to stakeholders a forward-looking, values-driven approach.

As a result of this complexity and vested political interests, electoral development and reform typically take time and are not linear. It can take several cycles for election processes to improve, and there may be steps backward as well as forward. In order to minimise the back-steps, we need to look at how our actions today will affect long-term electoral development so that short-term interests don't jeopardise democratic growth.

It can be helpful to focus on promoting the mechanisms and dynamics that support ongoing change and reform. These can help strengthen the potential for long-term development with the re-calibration of election processes through successive election cycles. This involves prioritising the strengthening of 1) accountability (through transparency and effective scrutiny by observers, the media, academics, and the public), 2) institutional engagement with stakeholders (particularly by the election administration), 3) a learning approach (that promotes institutional responsibility and adaptation), 4) judicial checks, and 5) an active citizenry.

Citizen assemblies on election reform could be utilized in the future to promote citizen-centred electoral development. Citizen assemblies have the potential to add substantively and persuasively to the dialogue on election development and reform and to help political and election administration leadership be more accountable and more centred on public interest and preferences. They can help by looking at the complexities of election reform and focusing on the long-term interests of the people of a country rather than the immediate gains for parties or institutions. To be effective, they need to be mandated by authorities with an obligation on parliament and the election administration to consider and publicly respond to recommendations made.

Shortcomings in Practice in International Support

At the ground level, we see various shortcomings with international support in practice, including international interest coming late and often just at the time of an election. People often wake up to the risks just before election day, but reform does not happen so fast. Time is needed to undertake a positive and inclusive process of legislative reform and for changes to then be put into practice. Time is needed to strengthen institutions, for example, for election administrations to become more independent and accountable and for new election commissioners to be appointed and established. By-elections can also provide a useful opportunity to develop practice and measure progress (or lack thereof). So political and development support is needed throughout the electoral cycle, from one election to the next and over several cycles.

In particular, civil society needs to have ongoing rather than periodic financing. We rely on citizen observers to provide comprehensive scrutiny and to advocate for reform between and over election periods. They need to have continuity of funding to be effective in the critical period between elections. They can have a far greater reach than international observers, with a larger presence and covering more stages of an election process. It is a very hard job that they do, often with considerable personal risk. Citizen observers are a key frontline accountability check on election processes.

Another shortcoming in practice can be diplomatic hesitancy in being clear about electoral deficiencies. Such hesitancy has obvious immediate benefits in maintaining relationships with counterparts. However, not being clear about problems has longer-term risks. It can make the international community look naïve, weak, and complicit in corruption. It can alienate losing parties (who may come to power one day). It can also leave citizens frustrated, risking further disillusionment with democracy. Thus, for short-term gains, it may be that electoral accountability is undermined and reputations diminished. Not being clear about electoral problems in private or public messaging may, therefore, be seen as a high-risk strategy in the long run, contributing to the erosion of democratic values.

Credible international and citizen election observers can provide reliable information and balanced public commentary.[5] Deployment of

---

[5] Organizations undertaking credible international election observation have endorsed the Declaration of Principles for International Election Observation, intro-

substantive observer missions enables the diplomatic community to be better equipped with information and to have public reporting on which to base their own commentary. Credible election observation identifies compliance with a country's international commitments and also shortcomings and makes recommendations for reform. While each mission is independent, there is an increasing onus on a collaborative approach between missions to increase effectiveness.

Negative commentary from observer missions may not be welcomed by a host country, but such scrutiny is part of democratic accountability and strengthening. It is an investment in long-term democratic growth. It is also advantageous for diplomats, as independent entities are documenting and giving public commentary on election processes (which may involve considerable backlash), to which diplomatic commentary can refer.

In contrast, diplomatic watch activities undertaken by embassies over the election-day period provide some insight but are limited. They

---

duced under the auspices of the United Nations in 2005. The Global Network of Domestic Election Monitors and the Declaration of Global Principles for Nonpartisan Election Observation and Monitoring by Citizen Organizations are open for organisations undertaking credible citizen observation.

enable diplomats to gain some first-hand sense of an election process, but this is only part of any election, with major stages taking place before and after election day (including the registration of voters and candidates, campaigning, and complaints and appeals processes). While observers seek to be comprehensive, diplomatic watch involves seeing a very limited number of polling stations, typically in urban hubs and often only during daylight hours, without seeing the results or tabulation process (which are as critical as the voting).

Capitals are at times impatient to issue congratulatory statements. However, problems with an election process can sometimes be hard to see and take time to emerge. Therefore, it can be prudent to wait, to refer to credible observer reports, and to use measured and cautious language rather than making conclusive statements on the process.

Conclusions for the Diplomatic Community

Engaging in elections provides an opportunity to promote positive electoral processes and democratic growth, but the risk of negative exposure also needs to be considered. It can be easier and less exposing to work collaboratively with other diplomatic entities when challenging stakeholders, providing technical support, and being critical about an electoral process. It can also mean that there is an established collective mechanism in place that enables faster engagement and responses should an election become problematic. It can be helpful if like-minded ambassadors engage early with key stakeholders to promote democratic responsibility and actions. Risks in international development cooperation can also be mitigated by providing support not just to institutions but also to the checks and balances in an election process (which provide the mechanisms for ongoing change).

To conclude, there is a need to take a long-term citizen-centred approach. This means listening not just to those with power (who may want to entrench), but also to civil society, academics, opinion polls, and possibly also to citizens' assemblies. It means supporting the checks and balances in an electoral process that are there to protect citizens' interests. Future generations also need to be served, so actions should balance the short-term needs of the moment with the longer-term interests of those that will follow us.[6]

---

[6] For more information on intergenerational equity see Principles of Effective Governance for Sustainable Development, endorsed by the UN Economic and Social

Active, consistent, and smart diplomatic engagement in elections can help promote democratic renewal. This requires diplomatic skills in promoting the democratic responsibilities of all actors throughout the election cycle, in being critical when warranted, and in supporting the guardrails that make an election and democracy meaningful. While it is easier to talk in generalities about democracy, there is now more than ever an imperative to be clear about electoral shortcomings and smartly support long-term citizen-centred election development.

About the autor

Hannah Roberts is an independent governance consultant focusing mainly on elections since 1999. In election observation and assessment Hannah Roberts has been Head of Mission for the OSCE (in Canada, Afghanistan, and Finland), and Deputy Chief Observer for the EU (in Kenya, Nigeria and Pakistan). She has run out of country voting (including for the South Sudan referendum in Europe), undertaken technical assistance with election commissions, worked with civil society organizations, and planned and evaluated electoral and parliamentary assistance

---

Council in 2018.

programs. Hannah Roberts has helped develop election observation methodology with the EU and the OSCE, and has contributed to various publications.

Protecting Democracy in the Digital Age

Idayat HASSAN

The internet has provided unprecedented access to vast amounts of information to its more than 5 billion global users. It has revolutionized communication as people can now connect, share, and receive information from all over the globe almost instantly. Social media platforms have furthered these connections and can, when used for good, contribute positively to enhancing the democratization of governance systems by enabling citizen groups to organize and hold elected officials accountable and promote civic education efforts across countries and even regions.

However, for all the positives brought by the growth of this online ecosystem, there are still many issues to be addressed. Disinformation, different from misinformation in its deliberate intent to mislead, aims to either delegitimise institutions, groups or personalities, glorify a leader or, during elections, confuse voters, instigate voter apathy or marginalise women and other vulnerable groups. While information disorder is not a new phenomenon, the current phase is more challenging given the scope of the manipulation, the ease with which information can be shared and the multiplicity of techniques adopted to do so. The "democratization" of information disorder has also seen a proliferation of actors, including individuals, state actors, foreign governments, and specialist firms, who can reach a mass of audiences. Thriving online, these manufactured falsehoods pose a threat to democracy or democratic structures.

How Information Disorder is Affecting Democracy

Information disorder is enabling authoritarian regimes to set and control a narrative that reinforces their governance approach, sow confusion and undermine democratic movements. Promoters and members of authoritarian states work to glorify the merits of illiberal governments in key areas of governance and development. They argue that economic growth is higher in authoritarian states, with reference regularly made to the way China has been able to lift millions out of poverty. They also push the narrative that the incapability of democratic systems and their inability to address the challenges and reach consensus timely – due to their participatory structures – stymie wider development progress. Despite both notions being challenged by the available evidence, information disorder has been weaponized by authoritarian governments to advance regime continuity through the disruption of credible flows of information to citizens and the deliberate spread of disinformation.

Another way of controlling the narrative is to close the space. Internet shutdowns are increasingly used by authoritarian states to clamp down on alternative narratives, even though evidence suggests they disrupt economies, violate human rights, endanger livelihoods and shield governments from legitimate scrutiny and criticism. Regulation and legislation to tackle disinformation are also growing in prominence, though their misapplication in authoritarian contexts can further limit the space for freedom of expression by targeting certain groups. In short, strategies range from the crude to the sophisticated and from the methodical to the makeshift, but each serve to close off or toxify social media platforms as a space for sharing and discussing information and opinions.

In the area of peace and security, information disorder is pushing citizens into polarized echo chambers that are further breaking down the social fabric and fuelling hostility and violence. False information spread online in India, Myanmar, Nigeria, Bangladesh, and Mali, to give just five examples, led to outbreaks of violence along religious and ethnic lines. Armed non-state actors are also exploiting the disinformation ecosystem to recruit, expand, and organize in ways that undermine democracy. In northeast Nigeria, the Islamic State in West Africa Province has created propaganda to promote itself as a credible alternative to the Nigerian state, which it portrays as an aggressor through videos and images of soldiers being defeated by the ragtag Islamist army.

Disinformation efforts are also stymying efforts to promote gender equality. Women in, or seeking to participate in, political life are increasingly faced with campaigns that attack them for doing so. It is usual to see aspersions cast on a woman's reputation and capacity to prevent them from participating both in politics and, in the worst cases, casting their vote. In the United States, for example, the intentional leakage of Hillary Clinton's personal information and gendered disinformation targeting the track record and route to power of Vice President Kamala Harris, tell a story that is similar across the globe. From Nigeria to Brazil, women in politics have been tainted by disinformation that attacks their credibility or person using deep fakes, altered pictures or false narratives.

Information disorder is also impinging on the right to privacy, a fundamental human right guaranteed by international human rights instruments, including the International Covenant on Civil and Political Rights. But the lack of robust legislation and enforcement capacity in developing countries has enabled the collection of personal data by tech companies and different actors for sale to the highest bidder.[1] This information has a whole range of uses, including for political mobilisation. Facebook's entire operating model is based on collecting and then selling its users' data, primarily to advertisers. But some of this data can be, and has been, handed over to governments and law enforcement agencies when requested. This is potentially problematic in states where investigative institutions are politically partisan or seek to clamp down on dissenting voices.

Digital intrusions into private data are furthered by the growing interest in mass surveillance of

---

[1] https://tacticaltech.org/news/personal-data-political-persuasion/.

the internet and phones. Many countries across the world are moving towards a Chinese-style model of digital authoritarianism. India, Indonesia, Belarus, Iran, Jordan, Morocco, Saudi Arabia, Nigeria and South Africa have all sent delegations to better understand how China's internet firewall works.[2] Others – such as Saudi Arabia, Eritrea, Ethiopia, Iran, and China – are using the premise of the threat of disinformation to introduce laws to silence online dissent. Freedom House's annual Freedom on the Net study found internet freedom to be in decline, with significant deterioration in 30 countries, including Myanmar, Uganda and Belarus. All 30 countries highlighted are either authoritarian states or hybrid regimes.[3]

Finally, disinformation is becoming a factor shaping election processes across the world. Falsehoods can be curated by international experts, troll farms or groups of domestic actors keen to push a political agenda. They have been used to confuse voters by overwhelming them with vast amounts of conflicting information, to

---

[2] https://arabcenterdc.org/resource/mapping-digital-authoritarianism-in-the-arab-world/ see also https://freedomhouse.org/report/freedom-net/2018/rise-digital-authoritarianism.

[3] https://www.wgbh.org/news/2017/11/02/myanmar-fake-news-spread-facebook-stokes-ethnic-violence.

attack the credibility of political opponents or the election management body, and to even reduce voter turnout in opposition areas on election day. The latter was documented in Kano state, Nigeria in 2019, where falsehoods about polling station violence circulated early on voting day.[4]

More sophisticated micro-targeting approaches – tapping into available user data to send specific content tailored to a specific user, as was seen in the 2020 US election – are also a growing phenomenon that will only increase as the digital space becomes increasingly influential in electoral campaigns. But capturing and documenting these growing threats to a core tenant of democracy remains in its infancy. Key election stakeholders are not yet inoculated on how to tackle disinformation, and in most cases, observation missions remain focused on traditional areas of coverage, with insufficient recognition of the way technology and information disorder can impact the campaign and the voting process.

---

[4] Hassan, I & Hitchen, J. (2020). "Driving division? Disinformation and the new media landscape in Nigeria". Centre for Democracy and Development.

Digital Platforms, Approaches, and Actors

WhatsApp and Facebook are the most common digital platforms used, but other channels such as YouTube, Instagram, Twitter and Tik Tok have significant numbers of users. However, to understand how information moves online requires an understanding of the interconnectedness of these social media platforms. Conversations that take place on WhatsApp, for example, may subsequently become a topic for debate on Twitter, with tweets then screenshotted and shared across Facebook. Social media platforms remain the most common tools used in influence operations. They support a wide array of approaches for the sharing of mis/disinformation, which are laid out below:

- **Computational propaganda and the automation of content are growing features of the online disinformation industry.** Botnets, groups of bots and coordinated groups of trolls – called troll farms – promote specific narratives and are deployed to generate online conversation and get stories trending. They use pre-agreed hashtags and share each other's content through "mutual admiration societies". Small click farms and troll factories have sprung up across the region to amplify their message and harass opponents.

- **Astro turfing.** This involves unsolicited comments on social media networks, often by political consultants.
- **Microtargeting.** This uses consumer data to create and target specific geopolitical locations and interests, biases and religious groups.
- **Deep fakes.** These are digitally altered or fabricated videos or audio that are increasingly sophisticated.
- **Shortened URLs.** These are used by disinformation peddlers to direct unsuspecting victims toward spreading disinformation from fake sites.
- **Doctored chyrons.** These are electronically generated captions superimposed on a television or cinema screen. These images and logos can be used to misrepresent pictures and videos.
- **Masking online identities.** This involves obscuring one's online identity through the use of proxy and troll accounts, usually in order to anonymously spread disinformation.
- **Manipulated audio, pictures, and videos.** This involves the digital alteration of social media content to fit a specific agenda.

The interconnected nature of online platforms is also reflected in the increasing overlap between online and offline sources of information. Increasingly, conventional media picks up information from social media to broadcast across offline channels. In other instances, information from conventional media such as television, radio, and newspapers becomes digitised and is shared online. This trend is prevalent across the world, though there are geographical differences. In the developing world, the often forgotten but salient vector in influence operations are the unregulated local tabloids, which are used, often by political actors, to shape community views, values, and beliefs or to propel propaganda to a wide and broadly receptive audience.

Actors behind the increased flow of falsehoods include national and foreign governments, political parties, political consultancies, security agencies, media houses, individual influencers, ethnic and religious groups, and even grassroots movements. Increasingly, disinformation disorder is a global operation and a business. In Nigeria, young influencers produce fake news on demand at a cost of US$ 100 per month[5], whilst in Belgium, the company Media Vibes SNC owns over 180 URLs devoted to creating and spreading fake news. Furthermore, the company provides applications for people to develop and

---

[5] https://iit-techambit.in/fake-news-the-newelection-rigger/.

spread their own fake news online in a "do-it-yourself media" model.[6]

The motivation for manipulating information varies, with some actors doing it for financial gain or to maintain political influence, whilst others may seek to push a particular agenda. Often, significant events such as elections, protests, insecurity or natural disasters serve as a pretext for manipulating information. It is also worth pointing out that there is a lack of political will amongst elites towards quelling disinformation because, in some instances, they stand to benefit from it.

Tackling Disinformation and Promoting Democracy

Disinformation is being used to shrink and silence opposing voices, delegitimize institutions and personalities and suppress voter turnout and participation in elections. Even when it does not have a direct impact, the volume of information in the public domain and the difficulty in discerning what is true and what is not are impacting citizens' trust in institutions and public figures. The response of citizens to even valid

---

[6] https://iit-techambit.in/fake-news-the-newelection-rigger/.

news is to regard it with cynicism because of the polluted information ecosystem. The confusion and mistrust being sown by disinformation is undermining democracy and engendering pre-existing divisions in many societies. Information disorder is also hampering adherence to and enforcement of the rule of law.

Information disorder has found the space to thrive, in part because of a wider democratic decline. The Freedom in the World report for 2022[7] illustrated that countries with aggregate score declines have outnumbered those with gains every year for the past 16 years. This has contributed to citizens' lack of access to information, poor economic indicators, clampdowns on rights, and weak and pliable institutions. This suggests that dealing with disinformation should not be limited to creating laws, better engaging technology partners or delivering digital literacy, but that it always must find ways to improve and strengthen wider participatory and democratic structures and frameworks, alongside regulation.

Responses to information disorder should also prioritize the origin and spread of falsehoods. Understanding what is allowing disinformation

---

[7] https://freedomhouse.org/sites/default/files/2022-02/FIW_2022_PDF_Booklet_Digital_Final_Web.pdf.

to grow and what is facilitating the spread – in many cases, a declining trust in democracy – can shape efforts to engage with citizens and empower them to take up the fight against fake news at an individual level. Regulating social media – at both state, regional and international levels – still has a role to play, and this is increasingly being discussed, proposed, and implemented by states and international bodies. However, keeping politics out of these discussions at the national level is important, if difficult, to avoid regulation being used to threaten free speech and curb criticism, particularly in already authoritarian or hybrid states.

The owners of social media companies also have a responsibility to do more. They collect personal data from people provided online and sell it to advertisers. They are also making profits from personal data and regularly provide information and comply with requests from authoritarian, semi-authoritarian, and hybrid governments to censor or remove content that those governments consider "fake news". Yet their ability to ensure that disinformation is not circulating on their platforms is limited and varies significantly depending on where in the world you reside. There has been talk about setting out common rules across social media platforms to moderate content. The need for global standards fashioned based on democratic norms and fundamental human rights rooted in universal values is clear. However, to be effective, any moderating standards should not just adhere to local ethos and values but, more importantly, must be rooted in local nuances.

About the Author

Idayat Hassan is the director of the Centre for Democracy and Development (CDD), an Abuja-based policy advocacy and research organization that focuses on deepening democracy and development in West Africa. She is a lawyer by profession and has had fellowships at many universities across Europe and the USA. Idayat Hassan has consistently improved the CDD's position as a civic tech leader with a portfolio of projects and has fostered the advance of research through quite modern methods, e.g., using an app to identify electoral fraud and analysing the use of personal data in political campaigning in Nigeria. She is without doubt one of the most accomplished experts in the region and is regularly quoted by relevant media outlets such as the Washington Post, BBC or the Economist.

Spheres of Action in a Divided World

Bruno MAÇÃES

World Order

In his speech on the annexation of the occupied provinces in Ukraine, Russian President Vladimir Putin described a global system of rules imposed by the West and proclaimed that Russia "is not going to live by such makeshift, false rules". His starting point is the belief that Russia cannot be Russia under the existing world order. By the same token, under those rules, the Russian president cannot truly be the Russian president. He proposes to redesign the rules. "Where did that come from anyway? Who has ever seen these rules? Who agreed or approved them? Listen, this is just a lot of nonsense, utter deceit, double standards, or even triple standards!"

Sergey Karaganov, a foreign policy strategist close to the Kremlin, has called the Putin Doctrine "constructive destruction". As Karaganov puts it, Russia wants to erase the existing global system, primarily by refusing to take part in it and play by its rules.

Is the war in Ukraine a clash of civilizations, as Samuel Huntington might argue? In fact, Huntington included Russia and Ukraine as founding members of the same civilization. Karaganov is a better guide here. What Russia is engaged in is a full rebooting or reprogramming of the world system. If there is a clash, it is a clash between plans or programs, with the main actors actively trying to change the way the world works or to access the global operating system.

If the first phase of the Russian plan consists in uniting the former Soviet or Tsarist lands, the next is openly described by those around Putin as the gradual dissolution of NATO, the main obstacle to Russian power. Meanwhile, as the Western system continues to steer towards moral, political, and economic degradation, other powers will take over the task of building a new system. The Kremlin believes Russia and China will see their positions strengthened. When the time comes to establish a new system of global security to replace the dangerously outdated existing one it must be done within the framework of a different project. Mikhail Remizov, a prominent Russian political scientist called this "intellectual decolonization".

Putin and his advisers assumed that Russian oil and gas were so indispensable to the normal functioning of the European economy that Russia had nothing to worry about if Putin decided to start a war. Russia, they had concluded, could dictate its own rules. By placing energy flows and trade firmly in the service of Russian war aims, the Kremlin abandoned the system of global economic liberalism. Its preferred alternative deserves to be called "war economy". Having taken control of at least some of the control switches of the global operating system, Putin convinced himself he could impose some changes. He could reprogram the rules, at least partially.

Oil and gas revenue would continue to flow to Russia, feeding its war machine. To be sure, Western democracies might attempt to ban energy imports, but would they have the ability to stop Russia? Could they live with higher energy prices? And would the rest of the world join those sanctions? If India and China continue to buy Russian oil and gas, the attempt might backfire.

As it stops playing by the rules and actively moves to reprogram the existing system, Russia faces the obvious challenge that the full force of the system can be deployed against it. Western democracies can access the control switches of the world computer and reprogram some of its rules with the express goal of limiting Russian actions and power. The Ukraine war is a revealing moment in the history of world-building. The global system suddenly appeared as a tool of power rather than a neutral framework of rules. There is some danger in this moment of revelation because a number of state actors in the developing world may themselves stop playing by the existing rules or even look for alternative systems of play.

Rather than going to war themselves, Western democracies have adopted a set of targeted economic tools designed to reduce the Russian threat to the existing system. In the cybernetic model adopted in my forthcoming book ("Masters of the Metaverse"), they might be compared to antivirus software or perhaps even the programs in the Matrix designed to terminate intruders. Weapons and technology transfers to Ukraine proved their ability to quickly redesign the game environment for Russia: Suddenly, the Russian armed forces had to face a different adversary, one they never expected and would struggle to overpower.

The current crisis is showing with admirable clarity that the global system is best understood as a form of programming rather than an order of natural exchanges. Some have root access, others do not, but that does not mean that a deliberate hack of the program will work as intended. While Russia broke the rules, the game itself changed. It moved one level up. The great game is a game whose purpose is to create the rules of the game.

Antithetical Values

The strategic issue today is which paradigm of international relations will ultimately prevail. On the one hand, we see a return to a vision of global politics as marked by a renewed competition for spheres of influence. This is the paradigm of national interests, and its defining characteristic is the absence of common or overlapping perspectives. On the other hand, however, their force has been weakened; it is still the case that common institutions and an integrated global economy dominate most relations between states. Globalization has not retreated, interdependence has intensified, and states still find it necessary to engage in multiple cooperative endeavors. The struggle to find common perspectives and ways to manage common challenges and problems continues unabated. It is perhaps less formalized, more chaotic and, as a result, its outcomes have become correspondingly uncertain or even unpredictable.

In the case of Russia, the rejection of European values is complete and definitive. In the first stage, Russian leaders still spoke approvingly of adopting modern European norms and standards, even if this was always combined with the assertion that a "common European home" would be multipolar and could not simply absorb Russia into existing structures. After the Ukraine war, the break is irreparable, and we must assume that Russia will "turn east" or become increasingly isolated, a much larger Iran at best.

In China the European Union and the United States face a different challenge. In the past, the belief that China would ultimately follow the adoption of a capitalist market economy with the corresponding conversion to liberal democracy helped define Western foreign policy. That particular illusion has long been abandoned. We realize much better now that even countries on the same modernization path may end up in very different places. On the one hand, the very idea of a modern society now appears to us as much more capacious than before. Its basic elements are compatible with a myriad of different ways of life. Even the path taken by Western societies could easily reveal junctures where different alternatives could have been pursued.

Chinese elites – and broader tendencies in Chinese public opinion tend to follow – implicitly believe that to move closer to Western values or to attempt to imitate the West in different areas would be tantamount to abdicating China's edge, opting to compete on territory defined by the West and therefore on terms clearly tilted in its favor. If in the 18th century, a Chinese emperor famously explained to a British ambassador that he had no need for Western goods, the view in China today is that the country has no need for Western culture, ideas and values.

Two issues stand out and will have critical consequences for relations between China and the West. First, on the question of reciprocity, the West now recognizes that China is unlikely to accept at home those norms of economic openness and market governance from which it benefits when its companies operate in the American and European markets. The difficulty here is that full reciprocity can only be established if the West renounces all pretenses to the universality of its own values and starts to exclude China from the purview of a system of norms once intended for all. Closing the borders to Chinese investment or applying new tariffs and regulatory barriers to Chinese exports on the grounds that China does the same may serve different purposes: It could be an attempt to influence China to change its ways or, on the contrary, a measure meant to protect Western markets from Chinese interests.

The second major issue is directly related to security and the role of international law. As China pushes its own national interest in such conflict areas as the South China Sea and its disputed border areas with India, the West has an important stake in defending the status of international law and rules-based methods for conflict resolution. However, the challenge in this case is that those positions will increasingly be impossible to defend without a corresponding intensification of conflict, including in the military sphere.

The United States would like to distinguish between those countries that adhere to the same values and those that do not. With like-minded states, competition should happen in the "economic domain", but with other states, competition is taken to the political level, where it should be conducted through "enforcement measures". Every year – political elites in Washington would argue – countries such as China steal intellectual property valued at hundreds of billions of dollars, an economic and security risk to which the

Spheres of Action in a Divided World

United States will respond with counterintelligence and law enforcement activities to curtail intellectual property theft by all sources, while exploring new legal and regulatory mechanisms to prevent and prosecute violations. This is a world where competition, not cooperation, is the predominant reality. Values are less the common perspective of all nations than a specific way of life targeted by one's enemies and adversaries. They are antithetical.

How does it happen that a country tries to refocus on its national interests while growing skeptical of the role of values in foreign policy? The history of American foreign policy over the past century is one of the gradual construction of a global system of rules and institutions. This system was always intended to be one suited to American interests. In other words, it was meant to be the system that the United States would like to see governing relations between states. There was an initial contradiction in this project, of course. The system promoted by the world's most powerful democracy was not to be a democracy in the sense that its structures benefited from equal and weighted input from all humankind. Is this the contradiction responsible for our current predicament?

In a way, the answer is yes. Countries such as Russia and China are quick to point out that the international system is tilted in favor of American interests. It calls for the maintenance of order by the only state capable of fighting two or three simultaneous wars anywhere on the planet. It is based on economic competition between major multinational companies, which are predominantly based in the United States, while capital flows to the dollar, which only one actor can print at will. When calling for a multipolar world, China and Russia fall into a contradiction of their own: Their call for democracy in the global community is not met by democratization at home.

China is a signal case of all the ambiguities behind the concept of a global community. The Chinese state and Chinese companies are able to benefit from the rewards of open trade and investment, but many of the reciprocal obligations are never delivered because Chinese authorities have no intention of applying those principles to their domestic sphere and may even attempt to convince other countries to break away from the existing world order. World politics will tend to become increasingly fractured between different constellations of interests, and as a result, the very notion of a global community may approach breaking point. The role of the United

States is, of course, critical: If the global system no longer works as intended, if more and more countries act autonomously from it, then Washington will be tempted to dismantle it and avoid paying its share of the costs and obligations.

If values are often underpinned by national interests, the reverse is no less true. One international actor that understands this very well is the European Union. Its way of doing politics is uniquely suited to an international system based on rules and common institutions. Officials in Brussels will readily concede that the Europeans would struggle to defend their interests in a world where the naked defense of the national interest was the only game in town. Perhaps paradoxically, the discovery that what the European Union once considered universal values are, after all, not universally shared may lead to a more activist foreign policy, as these values now need to be defended and promoted in a hostile environment rather than being absorbed more or less automatically by other actors.

Spheres of Action

Confusion continues to reign on the issue of decoupling. On the one hand, authorities in Washington and Beijing regularly announce new initiatives to limit the free flow of capital and technology between their two countries, and many other state actors are not far behind. Economic connections with Russia are being broken at breakneck speed, but in this case, the root cause is less what one might call decoupling than conflict: During conflict and war, economic and social links are severed for the very simple reason that they cannot take place under conditions of radical insecurity. Connections also break down inside countries during civil wars.

The model of the Cold War is often in the background, and, again, the underlying theory here seems a simple one. The conflict between the West and the Soviet Union during the Cold War made most exchanges radically insecure, and so they were largely discontinued. Conflict, not decoupling. There were exceptions, when state authorities on both sides were able to carve out special areas under some sort of mutual protection, such as energy links after detente.

However, we also talk of decoupling in cases of integration, which is where the concept becomes somewhat paradoxical. There is as of now no Cold War between China and the United States. A Cold War may yet develop, and in that case, many of the existing economic and social links will disappear.

Spheres of Action in a Divided World

The current situation, however, is peculiar. In some areas, such as microchips, integration is disappearing. In others, it is still flourishing. Chinese exports to the United States stand at record levels. American investment banks are rushing into China. Cultural exchanges remain strong. The two economies remain highly dependent on each other, and no one can see how they could safely be broken apart. Europeans actually complain that American energy companies prefer to export energy to China.

One can only make sense of the paradox by drawing a distinction between two levels of action: The geopolitical and the economic. At the geopolitical level, actors try to concentrate power and will build all kinds of barriers preventing their own leverage from flowing elsewhere. Advanced chips, for example, are a source of geopolitical power, so the priority is to prevent your geopolitical rivals from having access to them. In certain circumstances, energy might also rise to the geopolitical level. At the same time, integration is encouraged at the economic level: There are no questions of power when it comes to the production of footwear, toys, or chemicals. Whether Chinese companies win contracts to build a road somewhere in the world comes under the rules of economic competition, but *prima facie* there is no geopolitical question.

There is no such thing as decoupling in this context. There is, however, something quite new, which comes into view from a two-level perspective: The emergence of global industrial policy, with the concentration of power in the hands of state actors, which expect to use this power to shape the rules of the global economic system. The model of how countries work within their borders has now been replicated at the global level.

Whether decoupling in the sense of conflict can be prevented depends on the stability of the two-level game described in this essay. One could say that superpowers are those states capable of operating at the higher level, where rules are decided or determined. Every other state operates at a lower level, playing by the existing rules.

As the full force of the global system is deployed against Russia, the impact could be stabilizing in the sense that global actors once again recover the awareness that global relations have a certain governing structure. However, the war in Ukraine also shows the fragility of that structure: In a world where the rules are so radically open to change, we can expect renewed attempts to test the system or to act at the limit or beyond the existing rules.

However, allow me to sound an optimistic note. No matter how intense, the competition to set the global rules has certain stabilizing characteristics. First, it is highly dynamic: Like electoral processes at the domestic level, it can promise the loser at any given stage that there will be new opportunities to challenge the outcome in the future. Second, it is not exclusive: One can imagine that some rules will be shaped by certain states, while others could reflect other influences, and there is even the possibility of mixed influences. Be that as it may, what in my writings I like to call the "world game" is still relatively new. We must wait to see if the competition between China and the United States can take this general form or whether a new Cold War becomes inevitable.

As for the European Union, the lesson from recent events is not that its preferred model of global relations has failed but that it is one model among several, and the extent to which it can succeed in partly shaping outcomes depends on the exercise of power and influence rather than the automatic worldwide expansion of seemingly universal values. Over the past two or three years, the European Commission has introduced what some commentators call a "Copernican Revolution" in its approach to the global order. Rather than expecting other major actors to converge on policies deemed universal in theory and practice, the Commission now wants to adopt certain policies unilaterally and design them in such a way that they will have an impact on global relations no matter what other actors choose to do. By applying the same competition laws to Chinese companies that it applies to European companies, for example, the European Union can tilt the global landscape in the direction of less state control and interference over economic relations.

In this new landscape, smaller states are not without their own sphere of action. I see two main ways in which they can actively adapt to the new reality of a fragmented world order. Firstly, they can bandwagon with larger states and lend their support to specific constellations of values and rules whenever they feel these values and rules are preferable to the alternatives. In this sense, neutrality is today much harder to defend. The very concept of a neutral set of rules governing global relations has become implausible. Secondly, and often simultaneously, smaller states can develop the adaptability and flexibility to thrive under a changing global environment. The mark of success in a fragmented world order is not whether you can thrive under a particular set of rules but whether you have the capacity to adapt to different rules in a world where nothing remains fixed for too long.

About the Author

Bruno Maçães is a Portuguese public intellectual and author. He studied at the University of Lisbon and Harvard University, where he wrote his doctoral dissertation under Harvey Mansfield. From 2013 to 2015, he was the Secretary of State for European Affairs of Portugal. He is a consultant and prolific commentator and writer. Among his books are The Dawn of Eurasia: On the Trail of the New World Order, History Has Begun: The Birth of a New America and Geopolitics for the End Time: From the Pandemic to the Climate Crisis.

Democracy Promotion Through Power-Sharing: The Role of Mediators' Constitutional Templates

Daniel BOCHSLER & Andreas JUON

Introduction

Power-sharing is widely considered as the most influential constitutional prescription for divided societies struggling to attain stability and democracy (Lijphart 1977), in particular after civil conflicts (Walter 1997). Political scientists conceive power-sharing as a comprehensive package of constitutional norms whereby all relevant groups in divided societies are to share political power. As power-sharing has inspired constitutional design across the world, scholars speak of an emerging global norm of political inclusion (Gurr 2002; Jenne 2007; Wimmer 2015). Power-sharing is widely advocated by peace-building practitioners (Bogaards 2000; Goetschel 2011) and has been institutionalized as a standard UN conflict mediation tool (McCulloch and McEvoy 2018).

The basket of constitutional norms addressed as power-sharing consists of guarantees that all relevant groups are represented across political institutions (most notably, in the parliament, government, and public administration). Moreover, it often encompasses political autonomy for minorities, for example through federalism (Lijphart 1977). Together, these constitutional norms aim to create a political culture whereby elites engage in compromise across ethnic or cultural divides.

While power-sharing is widely propagated by scholars and policymakers alike, it by no means forms a standardized, "one-size-fits-all" constitutional model (Bogaards 2019). Instead, there is a wide variety of arrangements that are often subject to intense negotiation. For example, in post-Hussein Iraq, the US-led transitional administration was convinced that the inclusion of Sunni and Kurdish minorities into government and their provision with autonomy was necessary to foster a transition to stable, democratic rule. However, there were intense debates on how to design the new Iraqi state's foundational constitution to achieve these aims, most importantly as regards the composition of the Iraqi Presidency and the drawing of federal administrative boundaries (McGarry and O'Leary 2007).

In this chapter, we shed light on the actors that design specific constitutional power-sharing rules and which factors shape their choice of its specific constitutional form. In particular, we highlight the role of external mediators, in the context of peace negotiations, and their footprint on the power-sharing rules contained in post-conflict constitutions. We argue that where mediators *themselves* have previous experience with power-sharing rules, they will be more likely to advocate them during mediation efforts as well. Moreover, they will choose its specific constitutional form in accordance with the constitutional templates available to them through their own experience.

We investigate these arguments quantitatively using original, global data on constitutional rules of power-sharing and international mediation efforts between 1946 and 2013 (Juon and Bochsler 2022). In accordance with our argument, we find that where countries are "exposed" to mediators that have past experience with corporate or liberal power-sharing constitutions, they become more likely to subsequently "shift" towards the same type of power-sharing as well.

We proceed as follows: In the next section, we present our theoretical argument. Next, we introduce our data. The fourth and fifth sections present the results of the statistical analyses and cases of application. In the conclusion, we highlight the political relevance of our findings.

Theory

We contribute to two facets of the literature on institutional engineering: First, we shed light on the type of constitutional power-sharing rules that are introduced in post-conflict contexts. And second, we highlight learning processes from foreign countries, focusing on the role of external mediators.

Scholars speak of institutional engineering when constitutional norms related to the main political organs of the state are chosen purposefully to engineer desirable outcomes (Sartori 1968). In the context of divided or post-conflict countries, political scientists primarily prescribe power-sharing with the aims of achieving political integration, stability and democracy (Lijphart 1977, 30; Horowitz 2003; Graham et al. 2017; Hartzell and Hoddie 2020). To achieve these purposes, power-sharing is underpinned by three inclusive constitutional pillars at the central state level: Proportional representation of all relevant groups in parliament, provisions for grand coalitions or executive power-sharing, and minority veto rights (Lijphart 1977). These are often complemented by a fourth pillar at the subnational level, group autonomy, but the latter is excluded from the present analysis because of persistent findings according to which the factors explaining the introduction of autonomy rules and their political consequences widely differ from the first three pillars (cf. Juon and Bochsler 2022).

For the three pillars of power-sharing at the central state level, constitution-makers have a wide variety of different institutional possibilities to choose from (Bogaards 2019; Lijphart 1977). To facilitate our discussion, we group these into two major types. A first type, corporate power-sharing, "accommodate[s] groups according to ascriptive criteria, such as ethnicity or religion" (McGarry & O'Leary, 2007: 675). For instance, Kosovo's constitution lists the specific minority groups that have representation rights in parliament. Usually, corporate rules also foresee reserved seats in government for privileged groups and veto rights over legislation. Such corporate rules have been widely used to promote transitions to peace and democracy, most notably in Bosnia, Lebanon, Kosovo, and Cyprus.

In contrast, a second, liberal type of power-sharing "rewards whatever salient political identities emerge in democratic elections, whether these are based on ethnic or religious groups, or on subgroup or transgroup identities" (McGarry & O'Leary, 2007: 675). They avoid a clear specification of the groups among whom power is to be shared and rely instead on encompassing constitutional rules. For instance, under the South African interim constitution after apartheid (1993-1995), the cabinet portfolios were distributed proportionally to parliamentary parties, in correspondence to the number of seats they held in parliament, assuring that no relevant social group was left out. This second type too, has been used in diverse contexts to support democratic and post-conflict transitions, most notably in post-Hussein Iraq, Fiji (1997-2008), and North Macedonia.

We now discuss how power-sharing has become a global standard prescription for post-conflict and divided societies and what influences their choice between its corporate and liberal alternatives. We focus on horizontal diffusion processes between sovereign states. As existing studies show, democratic and inclusive forms of government are transmitted via international norms (e.g., Starr 1991; Gleditsch and Ward 2006). However, as regards the diffusion of more specific constitutional rules, the available evidence remains more embryonic. Studies show that countries are influenced by their regional neighbors in their choice of electoral systems (Bol et al. 2015) and that there are geographical patterns in the diffusion of power-sharing practices more broadly (Cederman et al. 2018).

We proceed from the observation that, in states that are ethnically divided or affected by intractable conflict, power-sharing is a convenient and intuitively appealing solution (McCulloch and McEvoy 2018). However, oftentimes, reaching a compromise on its specific constitutional form is difficult. In this process, international mediators can help. In the short term, they may facilitate interactions between formerly opposed groups, generate trust between them and help them reach agreement on mutually beneficial power-sharing constitutions. In the long term, mediators may stabilize power-sharing constitutions by threatening diplomatic, economic, and coercive sanctions should one side seek to unilaterally alter or overturn them.

The choice of constitutional rules of power-sharing, then, depends both on the domestic political context of the host state and the actions of conflict mediators, along with other external actors. Domestically, constitutional choices are constrained by the government's expectations and preferences related to democratization, as well as structural features, such as ethnic groups' relative sizes, their political geography, and political strength. McGarry and O'Leary (2009, 72) assert that "most sensible consociationalists... eschew [corporate power-sharing] devices, and prefer liberal rules", expecting them to facilitate democratization (see also Lijphart 1995). Vice-versa, corporate power-sharing might offer more robust securities for the inclusion of specific groups (Lijphart 1995). Hence, corporate power-sharing is often preferred by moderately-sized ethnic minorities or weaker parties in civil conflicts that seek lasting guarantees for their well-being and security (Jarstad 2008; McCulloch 2014). Conversely, liberal power-sharing is more flexible and is often preferred by solid majority groups (Lijphart 1995; Jarstad 2008) and by smaller minorities that might be excluded from corporate power-sharing (Juon 2020).

Internationally, we highlight the preferences and experiences of the mediators *themselves*. The constitutional toolset that they recommend is influenced by the constitutional templates that are available to them, owing to their previous use in the mediators' "home" countries. In this vein, mediators whose "home" countries have previously used corporate (liberal) power-sharing will be more likely to advocate it in divided societies as well. We justify this expectation with reference to instrumental reasons (mediators have witnessed that these constitutional templates "work" in their own country), normative reasons (they have come to perceive these institutions as "appropriate" for diversity management (cf. March and Olsen 1989), and pragmatic reasons (the required institutional toolsets are "accessible" for them with little effort). Hence, they are more likely to prefer institutions they are familiar with and advocate similar solutions elsewhere.

We summarize these arguments in the following hypotheses:

Hypothesis 1: Countries are likely to adopt higher levels of corporate power-sharing following mediation attempts by mediators that have previous experience with corporate power-sharing.

Hypothesis 2: Countries are likely to adopt higher levels of liberal power-sharing following mediation attempts by mediators that have previous experience with liberal power-sharing.

Data and Variables

We examine these expectations quantitatively, relying on evidence from 130 countries around the world between 1946 and 2011.[1] Our dependent variables are each country's time-variant corporate and liberal power-sharing levels, as given by the Constitutional Power-Sharing Dataset (Juon 2020) and as introduced by Juon and Bochsler (2022). Mirroring Lijphart's (1977) concept of consociational power-sharing, these indices capture the degree to which each country provides a constitutionally enshrined grand coalition, proportional representation clauses, and mutual veto rights in the legislative process to ethnic minority groups. Ranging from 0 to 1, they provide a fine-grained operationalization of the degree to which a country employs such power-sharing provisions. Importantly for our purpose, these two indices differentiate between constitutional power-sharing provisions following the corporate and liberal logic, respectively.

To capture the impact of international mediators on power-sharing levels, we first identify whether a "host" state has been subject to *any* mediation attempts in the last 20 years, relying on existing datasets (DeRouen et al. 2011; Melander et al. 2009). Second, we measure the mediators' experience with corporate and liberal power-sharing, based on their home states' pre-

---

[1] We exclude full autocracies from our sample (polity index < -8).

vious constitutions (Juon 2020). For each host country, this results in an overall, time-variant index measuring to what degree it relied on expertise from either corporate or liberal power-sharing experts in the last 20 years (for details, see Juon and Bochsler 2022). These measures take the value 0 if no mediation was recorded in the last 20 years or if the mediators' countries never institutionalized power-sharing themselves. They approach 1 as more of the active external actors' countries had prior experiences with the respective type of power-sharing.

Quantitative Analysis

Our interest is in examining how the efforts of international mediators and their previous experience with power-sharing affect changes in a "host" state's power-sharing levels. For this analysis, we rely on a global sample of ethnically plural countries, for which we have analyzed power-sharing norms in the constitutions for the period of 1946-2013 (Juon 2020; Juon and Bochsler 2022). Our statistical analysis investigates constitutional changes within each country over time and the factors contributing to these changes.[2] While our focus lies on the role of ex-

---

[2] We rely on country-fixed effects, restricting our analy-

ternal mediators and their constitutional templates, we also take into consideration domestic factors that might affect the introduction of power-sharing (see Juon & Bochsler 2022 for details).

Table 1 shows our main results: The first and third models show our estimates for corporate power-sharing norms, and the second and fourth models for liberal constitutional norms of power-sharing. In the first two models, we run a placebo test, probing whether mediation efforts after domestic contestations by themselves engender systematic changes in the constitution. In models 3 and 4, we identify the specific mediators involved in these efforts and their experience with corporate (model 3) and liberal (model 4) power-sharing, thereby shifting focus to the constitutional templates available to them. Figure 1 visualizes the political influence of mediators, depending on their own experiences with power-sharing.[3]

We find no effect by mediation efforts by themselves (models 1, 2). However, in line with our

---

sis to within-country variation. We also employ year-fixed effects, whereby we control for secular time trends and concurrent global shocks.

[3] All our control variables were set to their mean, median or mode, respectively. We show our predictions for the range of observed values in our sample.

argument, we observe that the mediators' previous experience with power-sharing leaves a clear imprint on host states' constitutions. Host states subject to mediation efforts where the mediators' "home" countries themselves had previous experience with corporate power-sharing are more likely to shift towards higher levels of corporate power-sharing as well. Conversely, host states subject to mediation efforts by mediators from countries with liberal power-sharing substantially increase their own degree of liberal power-sharing as well.

Table 1. Model results

	Corporate PSI	Liberal PSI	Corporate PSI	Liberal PSI
	Model 1	Model 2	Model 3	Model 4
Mediation	0.023	0.019	-0.038	-0.057†
	(0.021)	(0.020)	(0.025)	(0.032)
Mediator corporate PSI			1.737†	
			(0.931)	
Mediator liberal PSI				0.481*
				(0.191)
GDP p.c. (logged)	-0.017	-0.041*	-0.013	-0.035*
	(0.012)	(0.016)	(0.012)	(0.015)

Population (logged)	-0.035	0.020	-0.042	0.014
	(0.049)	(0.025)	(0.049)	(0.023)
Nelda index	-0.004	0.073***	0.002	0.074***
	(0.007)	(0.012)	(0.007)	(0.012)
Fuel rents (log)	-0.002	0.003†	-0.001	0.003*
	(0.002)	(0.002)	(0.002)	(0.002)
Minority population %	0.037	-0.108*	0.050	-0.073*
	(0.061)	(0.047)	(0.055)	(0.035)
Post-conflict	-0.008	0.004	0.004	0.005
	(0.015)	(0.019)	(0.009)	(0.016)
Negotiated settlement	0.029	0.041*	0.027†	0.035*
	(0.019)	(0.017)	(0.016)	(0.014)
Battle-related deaths (logged)	0.0005	0.001	-0.002	0.00000
	(0.003)	(0.004)	(0.002)	(0.003)
Constant	0.322	0.412†	0.300	0.377†
	(0.308)	(0.224)	(0.307)	(0.210)
Country-fixed effects	yes	yes	yes	yes

Year-fixed effects	yes	yes	yes	yes
N	4756	4756	4756	4756
R-squared	0.802	0.717	0.817	0.733
Adj. R-squared	0.794	0.704	0.809	0.721
Residual Std. Error	0.076 (df = 4556)	0.076 (df = 4556)	0.073 (df = 4555)	0.074 (df = 4555)
F Statistic	93.022*** (df = 199; 4556)	57.884*** (df = 199; 4556)	101.892*** (df = 200; 4555)	62.569*** (df = 200; 4555)

†p<0.1; * p<0.05; ** p<0.01; *** p<0.001; country-clustered SE's in parentheses.

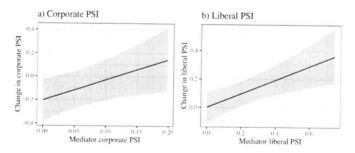

Figure 1. Influence of mediators' constitutional power-sharing templates on 'host' states degree of power-sharing (based on models 3 and 4).
Note: x-axis limited to range between minimum and maximum values of average mediator corporate and liberal power-sharing in our sample.

Institutional Engineering in Practice

We illustrate how mediators shape the diffusion of constitutional power-sharing rules with several specific examples. A first example is Burundi, which adopted a power-sharing constitution in 2004, aiming to stop a violent conflict between ethnic Hutu and Tutsi that claimed more than 300,000 lives between 1993 and 2005 alone (Mehler 2013). In Burundi, governing elites were nudged by external actors towards the adoption of power-sharing institutions, most notably by a team of South African politicians and diplomats who were involved in mediation efforts spanning several months (Mehler 2013; Samii 2013). Most notably, Burundi's constitutional provision that all parties with a vote share of more than 5% had to be proportionally represented in the cabinet (Constitution of 2004, article 129) closely resembled a similar clause in the 1993 South African constitution (article 88). Moreover, South African mediators also pushed for fixed ethnic quotas in the military, along the South African model (Samii 2013, 571).

A similarly central role of mediators influencing the adoption of specific types of power-sharing institutions can also be observed in numerous other cases. For instance, the member states of the NATO and EU clearly played a key role in shaping the introduction of power-sharing in post-Yugoslav states, including Bosnia and Herzegovina, Macedonia, and Kosovo (McCulloch and McEvoy 2018). Similarly, (transitory) liberal power-sharing institutions were imposed onto Iraq by the United States following their invasion of the country in 2004. And in a last-minute effort to prevent a looming external military intervention in the Comoros, South African mediators were able to successfully advertise power-sharing institutions there as well in 2000 (Mehler 2013).

Finally, turning a specific state that often engages in mediation during peace processes, we discuss the case of Switzerland (see the chapter by Simon Geissbühler in this volume). Switzerland is one of the established "classical" cases of power-sharing and one of the archetypes of liberal power-sharing specifically: Its historical Catholic minority gained its disproportional power indirectly through double majority rules, the bicameral parliament, and the federal organization of the state.

The Swiss Ministry of Foreign Affairs has long been actively involved in civil peacebuilding, which since 2004 has a legal basis. With Swisspeace, the government also sustains a research and policy institute for peacebuilding. Cases where Swiss mediators took leading roles in the negotiation of power-sharing constitutions include Burundi and Nepal (Comprehensive Peace Agreement of 2006, following a Maoist insurgency) (Greminger 2011, 19). However, these mediation efforts appear to have occurred with hardly any reference to the idea of institutional learning from the Swiss experience with power-sharing itself. Neither of the two constitutions has significant similarities to the Swiss power-sharing model. Moreover, senior diplomats describe the function of Swiss peacebuilding professionals as using their expertise to support the host states in order to find constitutional solutions suited to their specific political and social context (Greminger 2011, 18-9; Baechler and Frieden 2006). Reports by Swisspeace experts of power-sharing primarily refer to comparative expertise and evidence from post-war societies (e.g., Lanz et al. 2019; Raffoul 2019), and much less to the Swiss case (Iff and Töpperwien 2008).

These findings deviate from those offered by our statistical analysis. This suggests the need for future research to look beyond how the mediators' own experience with power-sharing informs their constitutional advocacy. Instead, it should also consider how their previous mediation experiences shape their subsequent constitutional recommendations, as in the Swiss case.

This highlights the need for more comparative qualitative evidence (further external actors and a longer timespan) and more nuanced evidence on the role that external actors play in the decisions leading to new constitutions in general.

Conclusion

In the scholarly literature and in the peacebuilding practice, "power-sharing" is employed as a wide concept, covering a variety of dimensions (Strøm et al. 2015) and types of constitutional provisions for political inclusion (McGarry & O'Leary 2007; McCulloch 2014). Contributing to the literature on institutional engineering and the origins of power-sharing (Wucherpfennig et al. 2016; Cederman et al. 2018), our chapter sheds light on the actions of external actors in post-conflict environments. It goes beyond earlier work, looking not only at the introduction of power-sharing, but also at the mechanisms leading to the introduction of specific constitutional provisions.

Our statistical analysis suggests strong diffusion effects, whereby mediators shape the choice of power-sharing in post-conflict contexts: Where countries are "exposed" to mediation efforts by mediators that have past experience with corporate or liberal power-sharing constitutions, they become more likely to subsequently "shift" towards the same type of power-sharing as well. Our results call for new research into the mechanisms at play and new research investigating the role of external actors in the constitution-building process.

This choice of constitutional rules is also politically highly consequential, as they have been subject to controversial debates on how they affect democracy. Empirical research indicates that power-sharing supports and bolsters various aspects of democratic quality as well (Bochsler and Juon 2021). The choice of the constitutional norms is crucial; therein entails trade-offs between various aspects of democratic quality (Lijphart 1995; McCulloch 2014; McGarry & O'Leary 2007; Bochsler & Juon 2021). Possibly, the choice of mediators in peace processes could thus also have indirect consequences for the future degree of political and social liberalism and the political rights of smaller groups.

Literature

Baechler, Günther, and Jörg Frieden (2006). "Nepal – Entwicklungszusammenarbeit und Konflikttransformation". *Schweizerisches*

Jahrbuch für Entwicklungspolitik 254 (2):189-209.

Bochsler, Daniel, and Andreas Juon (2021). "Power-sharing and the quality of democracy". *European Political Science Review* 13 (4):411-30.

Bogaards, Matthijs (2000). "The Uneasy Relationship Between Empirical and Normative Types in Consociational Theory". *Journal of Theoretical Politics* 12 (4):395-423.

– 2019. "Formal and Informal Consociational Institutions: A Comparison of the National and the Taif Agreement in Lebanon". *Nationalism and Ethnic Politics* 25 (1):27-42.

Bol, Damien, Jean-Benoit Pilet, and Pedro Riera (2015). "The international diffusion of electoral systems: The spread of mechanisms tempering proportional representation across Europe". *European Journal of Political Research* 54:384-410.

Cederman, Lars-Erik, Kristian Skrede Gleditsch, and Julian Wucherpfennig (2018). "The Diffusion of Inclusion: An Open-Polity Model of Ethnic Power Sharing". *Comparative Political Studies* 51 (10):1279-313.

DeRouen, Karl Jr, Jacob Bercovitch, and Paulina Popieszna (2011). "Introducing the Civil Wars Mediation (CWM) dataset". *Journal of Peace Research* 48 (5):663-72.

Geissbühler, Simon (2023). "Towards an Action-Oriented Democracy Diplomacy", In *Democracy and Democracy Promotion in a Fractured World: Challenges, Resilience, Innovation*, ed. S. 173, Geissbühler. Berlin/Zürich: LIT Verlag.

Gleditsch, Kristian S., and Michael D. Ward (2006). "Diffusion and the International Context of Democratization". *International Organization* 60:911-33.

Goetschel, Laurent (2011). "Neutrals as brokers of peacebuilding ideas?". *Cooperation and Conflict* 46 (3):312-33.

Graham, Benjamin A.T., Michael K. Miller, and Kaare Strøm (2017). "Safeguarding Democracy: Powersharing and Democratic Survival". *American Political Science Review* 111 (4):686-704.

Greminger, Thomas (2011). "Swiss Civilian Peace Promotion: Assessing Policy and Practice". Zürich: Center for Security Studies (CSS).

Gurr, Ted Robert (2002). "Attaining Peace in Divided Societies: Five Principles of Emerging Doctrine". *International Journal on World Peace* 19 (2):27-51.

Hartzell, Caroline A., and Matthew Hoddie (2020). *Power Sharing and Democracy in Post-*

Civil War States: The Art of the Possible. Cambridge: Cambridge University Press.

Horowitz, Donald L. (2003). "Electoral Systems: A Primer for Decision Makers". *Journal of Democracy* 14 (4):115-27.

Iff, Andrea, and Nicole Töpperwien (2008). "Power sharing. The Swiss experience". *Politorbis. Zeitschrift zur Aussenpolitik* 45 (2/2008):1-83.

Jarstad, Anna K. (2008). "Power sharing: Former enemies in joint government". In *From War to Democracy*, ed. A. K. Jarstad and T. D. Sisk. Cambridge: Cambridge University Press, 105-33.

Jenne, Erin K. (2007). Ethnic Bargaining. The Paradox of Minority Empowerment. Ithaca (NY): Cornell University Press.

Juon, Andreas (2020). "Minorities overlooked: Group-based power-sharing and the exclusion-amid-inclusion dilemma". *International Political Science Review* 41 (1):89-107.

Juon, Andreas, and Daniel Bochsler (2022). "The two faces of power-sharing". *Journal of Peace Research* 59 (4):526-42.

Lanz, David, Laurie Nathan, and Alexandre Raffoul (2019). "Negotiations, Continued: Ensuring the Positive Performance of Power-Sharing Arrangements". In *Special Report*.

Washington DC: United States Institute of Peace.

Lijphart, Arend (1977). *Democracy in Plural Societies. A Comparative Explanation*. New Haven: Yale University Press.

— (1995). "Self-Determination versus Pre-Determination of Ethnic Minorities in Power-Sharing Systems". In *The Rights of Minority Cultures*, ed. W. Kymlicka. New York, 275-87.

March, James G., and Johan P. Olsen (1989). Rediscovering Institutions. The Organizational Basis of Politics. New York: The Free Press, Collier Macmillan Publishers.

McCulloch, Allison (2014). "Consociational settlements in deeply divided societies: The liberal-corporate distinction". *Democratization* 21 (3):501-18.

McCulloch, Allison, and Joanne McEvoy (2018). "The international mediation of power-sharing settlements". *Cooperation and Conflict* 53 (4):467-85.

McGarry, John, and Brendan O'Leary (2007). "Iraq's Constitution of 2005: Liberal consociation as political prescription". *International Journal of Constitutional Law* 5 (4):670-98.

— (2009). "Power Shared after the Death of Thousands". In *Consociational Theory: McGarry and O'Leary and the Northern Ireland*

Conflict, ed. R. Taylor. London: Routledge, 15-84.

Mehler, Andreas (2013). "Consociationalism for Weaklings, Autocracy for Muscle Men? Determinants of Constitutional Reform in Divided Societies". *Civil Wars* 15 (S1):21-43.

Melander, Erik, Frida Möller, and Magnus Öberg (2009). "Managing Intrastate Low-Intensity Armed Conflict 1993-2004: A New Dataset". *International Interactions* 35 (1):58-85.

Raffoul, Alexandre W. (2019). "Tackling the Power-Sharing Dilemma? The Role of Mediation". Bern: swisspeace.

Samii, Cyrus (2013). "Perils or Promise of Ethnic Integration? Evidence from a Hard Case in Burundi". *American Political Science Review* 107 (3):558-73.

Sartori, Giovanni (1968). "Political Development and Political Engineering". *Public Policy* 17:261-98.

Starr, Harvey (1991). "Democratic Dominoes. Diffusion Approaches to the Spread of Democracy in the International System". *Journal of Conflict Resolution* 35 (2):356-81.

Strøm, Kaare, Scott Gates, B. A. Graham, and Havard Strand (2015). "Inclusion, Dispersion, and Constraint: Powersharing in the World's States, 1975-2010". *British Journal of Political Science*.

Walter, Barbara F. (1997). "The Critical Barrier to Civil War Settlement". *International Organization* 51 (3):335-64.

Wimmer, Andreas (2015). "Nation Building. A Long-Term Perspective and Global Analysis". *European Sociological Review* 31 (1):30-47.

Wucherpfennig, Julian, Philipp Hunziker, and Lars-Erik Cederman (2016). "Who Inherits the State? Colonial Rule and Postcolonial Conflict". *American Journal of Political Science* 60 (4):882-98.

About the Authors

Daniel Bochsler is an Associate Professor at Central European University (CEU), and a Full Professor at the University of Belgrade. His research interests include political institutions in heterogeneous societies, democratization, and elections. He conducts comparative analyses and studies on South-East European countries.

Andreas Juon is a Postdoctoral Fellow at ETH Zurich. He obtained his PhD from University College London in 2020. His research interests include power-sharing, territorial autonomy, and majority nationalist movements.

Country Examples

Towards an Action-Oriented Democracy Diplomacy Agenda

Switzerland's Democracy Assistance in an Era of Polarization and Authoritarian Resurgence

Simon GEISSBÜHLER

In an opinion poll conducted in May 2021, a whopping 93 percent of the respondents considered the mandate in Article 54 of the Swiss Constitution to promote democracy abroad "important" or "very important". 59 percent believed Swiss foreign policy should do "more" or "much more" to promote democracy – with a mere 4 percent opining that "less" or "much less" should be done in this regard. A massive 80 percent stated that the democratic tradition of Switzerland predestined Swiss foreign policy to promote democracy worldwide.[1]

This strong popular support for Swiss democracy promotion is linked to the positive connotation of Swiss democracy itself and the self-perception that democracy in Switzerland is a

---

[1] Opinion poll conducted by gfs.bern in May 2021, commissioned by the author; n=1,007.

unique case, a *"Sonderfall"*. While Swiss democracy functions like any other representative democracy – around 95 percent of the laws passed by parliament are never challenged by a referendum – it is reinforced and deepened by frequent popular initiatives (which are proposals for constitutional amendments) and referenda (which aim at canceling a law passed by parliament). These direct-democratic institutions of the Swiss polity are considered the cornerstone of Swiss exceptionalism and indeed a part of Swiss political identity. They are supported by an overwhelming majority of citizens independently of social strata, educational attainment, income, gender or party identification.[2]

Swiss Democratic Exceptionalism

While Swiss democratic exceptionalism is sometimes overhyped and has certainly some mythical features to it, it can be qualitatively and quantitatively discerned. Switzerland is "the world's

---

[2] Linder, Wolf (2010). *Swiss Democracy. Possible Solutions to Conflict in Multicultural Societies*. Houndmills, p. 92-127; Geissbühler, Simon (2015). *Die Schrumpf-Schweiz. Auf dem Weg in die Mittelmässigkeit*. Bern, pp. 43-53.

preeminent practitioner of direct democracy".[3] In no other country of the world are citizens asked to vote so often – on the federal, cantonal and municipal levels. The Swiss model is certainly not Athenian – but it gets closer to it than any other polity in today's world.[4] It puts a special emphasis on democracy as government not only for, but by the people.

The Swiss democratic system has its roots in early local proto-democratic governance and local participation in the Middle Ages and the liberal constitution of modern Switzerland of 1848. Since then, Switzerland has largely avoided internal strife and has been able to transform a relatively poor country lacking in resources into a prosperous one. The Swiss example shows that a complex, multi-layered democracy with referenda and initiatives can function rather well – as long as there are, among other prerequisites, sound civic education, responsible media, frequent political debates and deliberation among citizens and an appreciation for and political incentives to foster dialogue and compromise.

---

[3] Matsusaka, John G. (2020). *Let the People Rule. How Direct Democracy Can Meet the Populist Challenge.* Princeton/Oxford, p. 85.
[4] Garçon, François (2015). Democracy Close to the Classical Ideal, in Schwarz, Gerhard/Horn, Karen (eds.). *Watch the Swiss.* Zürich, pp. 42-44.

Swiss direct democracy has contributed to remarkable political stability and to both the legitimacy of the Swiss political system as a whole as well as the trust of citizens in the political process and institutions. Historically, direct democracy has helped to integrate a deeply divided society with cleavages along political, language, religious/confessional and cultural lines. Direct democracy reverts political decisions better to the median voter – also indirectly, as parties and the parliament tend to anticipate referenda and formulate policies and laws in such a way as to avoid them. Direct democracy has proven to be a powerful check, an instrument of permanent control in the hands of the voters. Finally, there is some empirical evidence to suggest that citizens in a direct democracy are more content than their peers in representative systems because they have more opportunities to get involved in and have an influence on the political process.[5]

---

[5] For a detailed discussion of the effects and outcomes of Swiss direct democracy see Vatter, Adrian (2007). Direkte Demokratie in der Schweiz: Entwicklungen, Debatten und Wirkungen, in Freitag, Markus/Wagschal, Uwe (eds.). *Direkte Demokratie*. Berlin: pp. 71-113; Geissbühler, Simon (2014). Does Direct Democracy Really Work? A Review of the Empirical Evidence from Switzerland, *Przegląd Politologiczny* 4: 87-97.

But, obviously, Swiss democracy is far from perfect. It excluded women for a very long time – to name just one example. It faces mostly the same challenges as all other democracies.[6] The Swiss experience also reminds us that "democracy is hard to achieve; yes, it is impossible to make perfect".[7] But democracy's imperfection might be one of the reasons to be optimistic about its future.

Why Then Isn't Switzerland a World Leader in Democracy Promotion?

Based on the largely positive experience with democracy, the constitutional and legal mandate to promote democracy abroad,[8] and the strong popular support for such policies, one would expect Switzerland to be at the forefront of global

---

[6] For a rather somber assessment of the state of Swiss (direct) democracy see Church, Clive H./Vatter, Adrian (2016). Shadows in the Swiss Paradise, *Journal of Democracy* 27(3): 166-175.
[7] Woodruff, Paul (2005). *First Democracy. The Challenge of an Ancient Idea*. Oxford/New York, p. 5.
[8] The constitutional mandate to promote democracy abroad is reiterated in the Federal Act on Measures pertaining to Civil Peace Support and the Promotion of Human Rights of 2003.

democracy promotion. However, this is not the case, mainly for the following four reasons.

First, there are important foreign policy principles standing in the way of a more active democracy promotion, namely Swiss neutrality and a tendency of foreign policy decision-makers to tread carefully and balance and counterbalance Swiss positioning in the international arena.

Second, there is a certain restraint in marketing the Swiss model. Because it is rather unique, many policymakers are reluctant to use it as a point of reference and to highlight it abroad. This fear is mostly unwarranted as nobody seriously advocates "exporting" a copy/paste model of Swiss democracy – something that would anyway fail.

Third, there is widespread unease with the term "democracy promotion" – even though the Swiss Constitution explicitly calls it that way. But the term has become "contaminated" by some military interventions in the 1990s and 2000s, which were led partly under the banner of promoting democracy. Even though one can easily argue that they had little to do with democracy promotion, the damage was done. Just as a side note: I use democracy promotion, support and assistance synonymously throughout this paper, also in lack of a better term.

Fourth, Swiss foreign policymaking is rather fragmented and polyarchic. While Switzerland is a medium-sized country in Europe with considerable soft power and globally well-connected economically, it is still among the smaller players on the international stage with limited influence on the great powers and the large political blocks and with constrained capabilities to scale up its foreign policy priorities.

This being said, Swiss foreign policy has done some valuable democracy promotion or assistance work – even though it has seldom been called like this and it clearly lacks an overarching strategic framework. There are four main lines of action. First, the promotion of decentralization, local participation and good governance, as well as capacity-building support for civil society, have been priorities of the Swiss Agency for Development and Cooperation (SDC) for many years – focusing on national/local ownership and long-term commitments.[9] As the contribution of Patricia Danzi in this volume explains SDC's approach in much detail, I don't need to be more specific here.

---

[9] Dahinden, Martin (2013). Democracy Promotion at a Local Level: Experiences, Perspectives and Policy of Swiss International Cooperation, *International Development Cooperation* 4.3.

Second, some valuable experts' work has been done to help design constitutional frameworks in fragmented, multicultural countries, taking into consideration and adapting the Swiss model of federalism, power-sharing and consociational democracy. The contribution of Daniel Bochsler and Andreas Juon in this volume underlines the potential of "democracy promotion through power-sharing".

Third, the participation of Swiss experts in election observation missions of the European Union, the Organization for Security and Cooperation in Europe (OSCE) and the Organization of American States (OAS) and concrete contributions to electoral integrity (e.g., through the negotiation of codes of conduct for political parties and electoral campaigns) have been a priority of Swiss foreign policy for many years.

Fourth, Switzerland contributes to what would be considered democracy promotion by its human rights diplomacy as outlined in the Guidelines on Human Rights 2021-24 – focusing on the freedom of expression, free media and the protection of minorities.[10]

---

[10] Swiss Federal Department of Foreign Affairs (ed.) (2021). *Guidelines on Human Rights 2021-24*. Bern.

A New Global Configuration and New Challenges to Democracy Assistance

Democracy promotion and its underlying analytical and strategic premises have needed some rejuvenation for quite some time.[11] Indeed, most experts and policymakers have long moved away from some of the obsolete democracy promotion policies and rhetoric of the 1990s and early 2000s, which focused almost exclusively (and wrongly) on elections as the panacea for everything. The geopolitical tectonic shifts in the last two decades have only highlighted the urgent need to question the old democracy promotion paradigms and dogmata.

Following the short unipolar moment after 1989, the world quickly entered into an era of heightened global polarization and rapid authoritarian resurgence. When some experts warned of the consolidation of authoritarian regimes and the coming of a global ideological, political, economic and strategic struggle between authoritarian and liberal powers,[12] many laughed them off as way too alarmist. But as Damir Marusic has pointed out (before the full-scale Russian attack

---

[11] Carothers, Thomas (2020). Rejuvenating Democracy Promotion, *Journal of Democracy* 31(1): 114-123.
[12] Kagan, Robert (2019). The Strongmen Strike Back, *The Washington Post* (17 March): A24-A27.

against Ukraine on February 24, 2022): *"It feels like the order we have all taken for granted since the end of the Cold War is badly decaying, and has gotten so fragile that it might well shatter soon. Worse than the decay itself, however, is what feels like our inability to perceive just how advanced it is"*.[13]

Clearly, the Russian war against Ukraine did not fall onto Earth like a meteorite from outer space.[14] It is first and foremost a symptom or a manifestation of the geopolitical tectonic shifts mentioned above. At the same time, it is the result of a cumulative parallel domestic and foreign policy radicalization in Russia. The reality is that Europe, too, has now left a short period of relative stability (whatever "stability" means), which was, in any case, rather an exception than the rule from a historical perspective. Europe has returned to a probably prolonged period of conflict and political, economic, strategic and ideological antagonisms.

Instead of mourning a reality and foreign policy recipes that no longer exist or no longer work, it is up to all policymakers and decision-makers to self-confidently and with foresight shape an

---

[13] Marusic, Damir (2021). The Coming Storm, *Wisdom of Crowds* (12 November).

[14] See, e.g., Bruno Maçães's article "Is Vladimir Putin Preparing for War?" in *The New Statesman* on 24 November 2021.

interest-driven foreign policy for the new (or not so new, but so far largely ignored) global realities. To mantra-like invoke the rules of the "old" international system and "values" won't do it. Clearly, some players in the system don't play by these rules anymore (if they ever have is another question). There is a need for a taboo-free analysis beyond the prevailing dogmata.

Talking about Switzerland, it is well understood that its foreign policy does not need to be overturned. It is well aligned and strategically solidly anchored. But there cannot be a "courant normal" either; Switzerland's foreign policy needs to be reconfigured in certain areas and aligned more realistically, more principled and more strongly with Swiss interests and values (which are the two sides of the same coin). One key field where such a reflection and readjustment has to take place is democracy assistance or support.

One of the consequences of the global tectonic shifts is the fact that democracy has become "embattled" globally.[15] Freedom House's data is clear: Democracy has been on the retreat worldwide for more than 15 years, and there has been a parallel "global expansion of authoritarian

---

[15] Plattner, Marc F. (2020). Democracy Embattled, *Journal of Democracy* 31(1): 5-10.

rule".¹⁶ While roughly half of the world's population lived in autocracies in 2010, this percentage has increased to over two thirds today. An excessively euphoric attitude towards democracy after 1989 rapidly tilted towards an equally distorted pessimistic one. It has become fashionable in democracies to talk bad about democracy.

Democracies are faced with a worrisome trend of weakening support for their institutions and increasing dissatisfaction with democracy itself. These trends are fomented by digitalization in general and social media in particular. Digitalization can shrink the democratic space through surveillance and worsen polarization; it can undermine democracy – and it is often used precisely to that end.¹⁷ Many democracies erode from within, but they are also under increased pressure from the outside – undermined and attacked relentlessly by the "sharp power" of authoritarian regimes.¹⁸ This outside pressure is ef-

---

[16] Freedom House (2022). *Freedom in the World 2022*. Washington.
[17] Tucker, Joshua A. et al. (2017). From Liberation to Turmoil: Social Media and Democracy, *Journal of Democracy* 28(4): 46-59.
[18] Walker, Christopher (2018). What is "Sharp Power"?, *Journal of Democracy* 29(3): 9-23; Walker, Christopher Walker et al. (2020). The Cutting Edge of Sharp Power, *Journal of Democracy* 31(1): 124-137; Beckley Michael/Brands, Hal (2022). China's Threat to Global

fective mainly because democracies are weakened from within.

At the same time, the global demand for democracy remains very high. In many countries around the globe, citizens fight for more freedom, participation and accountability of their leaders. The drive for democracy time and again comes from the grassroots and is anchored in local initiatives. Democracy's attractiveness often seems (albeit not always) inversely proportional: The more democratic a country is, the more complacent its voters and elites become. Many in democracies have withdrawn to the small amenities of life, looking at democracy as a given or even as a burden.

But democracies function and are resilient. Broadly based and legitimized decisions and the capability to self-correct have undeniable advantages. In the medium and long term, democracies have more stable and sustainable growth rates and economic policies than autocracies. Studies show that there is a significant positive correlation between democracy on the one hand and freedom, peace, development and innovation on the other.[19]

Democracy, *Journal of Democracy*.

[19] See, e.g., Olson, Mancur (1993). Dictatorship, Democracy, and Development, *American Political Science Review* 87(3): 567-576; Almeida, Heitor/Ferreira, Daniel

What to Do About It? Towards an Action-Oriented Democracy Diplomacy

Why should Switzerland care about global democratic recession? Why should it be in the business of democracy promotion in the first place? There are three main and interlinked reasons. First, Swiss foreign policy must care about democracy promotion because there is a constitutional and legal mandate to do so. Swiss foreign policy cannot limit itself to what has been done so far. The Swiss Foreign Policy Strategy 2020-23 explicitly stipulates that "Swiss foreign policy serves to both protect and promote freedom. This relates to Switzerland's self-assertion as a nation but also its confidence in promoting democracy, the market economy and the liberal international order".[20]

Second, it is in Switzerland's interest to support and promote democracy. It is an illusion to be-

---

(2002). Democracy and the Variability of Economic Performance, *Economics and Politics* 14(3): 225-257; Oneal, John R. (2003). Causes of Peace: Democracy, Interdependence, and International Organizations, 1885-1992, *International Studies Quarterly* 47(3): 371-393; Dodsworth, Susan/Ramshaw, Graeme (2021). Democracy's Development Dividend, *Journal of Democracy* 32(1): 126-138.

[20] Swiss Federal Department of Foreign Affairs (ed.) (2020). *Foreign Policy Strategy 2020-23*. Berne, p. 5.

lieve that "democracy in one country" is sustainable. It is also naïve to think that anything will happen or change by simply invoking the relevance and value of the "old" rules and institutions and by incessantly underlining that "we have to defend them". As Bruno Maçães and others have highlighted, the global system is no longer (and might never have been) "a neutral framework of rules".[21] We have to redefine these rules. It is evident that Swiss interests are better served when freedom, democracy and human rights are respected in Europe and beyond. Whenever freedom, democracy and human rights were under threat abroad, this had an indirect but often also a direct negative impact on Switzerland, as the country witnessed throughout its existence as a modern state since 1848.

Third, democracy is – as we have seen above – a key value anchored not only in the Swiss Constitution but also in the political DNA of the Swiss people. Defending this value and showing solidarity with and supporting those who strive for democracy or defend it makes sense and is politically and strategically coherent – as values are interests too, as Joseph S. Nye has so rightly un-

---

[21] Maçães, Bruno (2022). The New Geopolitics, *Project Syndicate* (29 July).

derlined.[22] To be very clear, supporting democracy abroad has nothing to do with hopeless idealism. The opposite is true: Values are an essential part of a well-understood, realistic foreign policy, as Swiss interests will be better served in a world in which democracy is respected.[23]

Swiss democracy promotion or assistance should first and foremost be a positive and active endeavor, not a defensive and reactive one. It is obviously not about exporting a copy/paste model of Swiss democracy. It is not only about inspiring others and showing solidarity but also about offering concrete support and tools and sustaining democratic resilience through development cooperation, peace policy programs and diplomatic efforts. The focus should be on concrete impact. In order to strengthen a coherent democracy diplomacy, the six following steps are needed.

First, Switzerland has to create a more robust strategic framework and narrative for a democracy diplomacy agenda – bringing the different threads together and politically valorizing and deepening the existing lines of action. This im-

---

[22] Nye, Joseph S. (2019). *Do Morals Matter? Presidents and Foreign Policy from FDR to Trump*. Oxford.
[23] For this argument see, e.g., Brands, Hal/Feaver, Peter (2017). Saving Realism from the So-Called Realists, *Commentary* 144(2): 15-22.

plies anchoring the issue better within the Swiss Federal Department of Foreign Affairs and its strategic documents and strengthening the intra- and inter-agency coordination.

Second, Switzerland has to define its "unique selling point" in democracy support, focusing on a few specific issues where it can realistically make a difference and have a measurable impact. It also has to think about new partnerships – for example, with the private sector.

Third, Switzerland has to mainstream democracy promotion in the large sense of the term better into its foreign policy and its politico-diplomatic messaging. It has to strengthen and diversify its relations with emerging democracies with which it shares common interests and that might be interested in sharing experiences.

Fourth, Switzerland is well placed to help shape a new narrative about democracy. While Switzerland is obviously too small to be a global "system operator" (see the chapter by Bruno Maçães in this volume), it should exert its influence. It can play a role in helping to re-center the democracies' efforts around a more optimistic, principled and positive approach – not so much against someone, but for democracy and its undeniable strengths.

Fifth, Swiss peace policy should – apart from its main focus on mediation, dialogue facilitation and long-term peace efforts – emphasize its politico-diplomatic and programmatic support for democratic resilience as a key element to sustainable peace.[24] While it is true that "democratic resilience" is still a relatively spongy concept in need of more theoretical and programmatic rigor,[25] it is safe to say that in order to strengthen democratic resilience, measures such as the support given to emerging and struggling democracies in general and to democratic parties and processes (e.g., electoral integrity, code of conducts for political parties), to local governance and decentralization (e.g., mayors, local participatory bodies), to institutions (e.g., free media) as well as to civic education in particular, are crucial. This is even more relevant today as studies show that "democratic resilience has become substantially weaker since the end of the Cold War".[26]

---

[24] Lührmann, Anna (2021). Disrupting the Autocratization Sequence: Towards Democratic Resilience, *Democratization*, 28(5): 1017-1039.

[25] Holloway, Josh/Manwaring, Rob (2023). How Well Does "Resilience" Apply to Democracy? A Systematic Review, *Contemporary Politics* 29(1): 68-92.

[26] Boese, Vanessa A. et al. (2021). How Democracies Prevail: Democratic Resilience as a Two-Stage Process, *Democratization* 28(5): 885-907.

Sixth, actions speak louder than words. Switzerland must lead by example and with conviction. It must continue to do its homework. Only then can it convincingly talk about democracy with and to others. As George Kennan wrote in his "Long Telegram" in 1946: "Much depends on health and vigor of our own society. [...] We must have courage and [self-confidence] to cling to our own methods and conceptions of human society".

About the Author

Ambassador Simon Geissbühler is a political scientist who joined the Swiss Federal Department of Foreign Affairs as a diplomat in 2000. He is currently heading the Peace and Human Rights Division. Opinions expressed here are solely his own.

Literature

Almeida, Heitor/Ferreira, Daniel (2002). Democracy and the Variability of Economic Performance, *Economics and Politics* 14(3): 225-257.

Beckley Michael/Brands, Hal (2022). China's Threat to Global Democracy, *Journal of Democracy*: https://www.journalofdemocracy.org/chinas-threat-to-global-democracy/.

Boese, Vanessa A. et al. (2021). How Democracies Prevail: Democratic Resilience as a Two-Stage Process, *Democratization* 28(5): 885-907.

Brands, Hal/Feaver, Peter (2017). Saving Realism from the So-Called Realists, *Commentary* 144(2): 15-22.

Carothers, Thomas (2020). Rejuvenating Democracy Promotion, *Journal of Democracy* 31(1): 114-123.

Church, Clive H./Vatter, Adrian (2016). Shadows in the Swiss Paradise, Journal of Democracy 27(3): 166-175.

Dahinden, Martin (2013). Democracy Promotion at a Local Level: Experiences, Perspectives and Policy of Swiss International Cooperation, *International Development Cooperation* 4.3: https://journals.openedition.org/poldev/1517?lang=de.

Dodsworth, Susan/Ramshaw, Graeme (2021). Democracy's Development Dividend, *Journal of Democracy* 32(1): 126-138.

Freedom House (2022). *Freedom in the World 2022*. Washington: https://freedomhouse.org/sites/default/files/2022-02/FIW_2022_PDF_Booklet_Digital_Final_Web.pdf.

Garçon, François (2015). Democracy Close to the Classical Ideal, in Schwarz, Gerhard/Horn, Karen (eds.). *Watch the Swiss*. Zürich, pp. 42-44.

Geissbühler, Simon (2014). Does Direct Democracy Really Work? A Review of the Empirical Evidence from Switzerland, *Przegląd Politologiczny* 4: 87-97.

Geissbühler, Simon (2015). *Die Schrumpf-Schweiz. Auf den Weg in die Mittelmässigkeit*. Bern.

Holloway, Josh/Manwaring, Rob (2022). How Well Does "Resilience" Apply to Democracy? A Systematic Review, *Contemporary Politics*: https://www.tandfonline.com/doi/full/10.1080/13569775.2022.2069312.

Kagan, Robert (2019). The Strongmen Strike Back, *The Washington Post* (17 March): A24-A27.

Linder, Wolf (2010). *Swiss Democracy. Possible Solutions to Conflict in Multicultural Societies*. Houndmills.

Lührmann, Anna (2021). Disrupting the Autocratization Sequence: Towards Democratic Resilience, *Democratization* 28(5): 1017-1039.

Maçães, Bruno (2021). Is Vladimir Putin Preparing for War?, *The New Statesman* (24 November): https://www.newstatesman.com/world/asia/2021/11/is-vladimir-putin-preparing-for-war.

Maçães, Bruno (2022). The New Geopolitics, *Project Syndicate* (29 July): https://www.project-syndicate.org/onpoint/the-new-geopolitics-rivalries-over-writing-the-rules-by-bruno-macaes-2022-07?barrier=accesspaylog.

Marusic, Damir (2021). The Coming Storm, *Wisdom of Crowds* (12 November): https://wisdomofcrowds.live/the-coming-storm/.

Matsusaka, John G. (2020). *Let the People Rule. How Direct Democracy Can Meet the Populist Challenge*. Princeton/Oxford.

Nye, Joseph S. (2019). *Do Morals Matter? Presidents and Foreign Policy from FDR to Trump*. Oxford.

Olson, Mancur (1993). Dictatorship, Democracy, and Development, A*merican Political Science Review* 87(3): 567-576.

Oneal, John R. (2003). Causes of Peace: Democracy, Interdependence, and International Organizations, 1885-1992, *International Studies Quarterly* 47(3): 371-393.

Plattner, Marc F. (2020). Democracy Embattled, *Journal of Democracy* 31(1): 5-10.

Tucker, Joshua A. et al. (2017). From Liberation to Turmoil: Social Media and Democracy, *Journal of Democracy* 28(4): 46-59.

Vatter, Adrian (2007). Direkte Demokratie in der Schweiz: Entwicklungen, Debatten und Wirkungen, in Freitag, Markus/Wagschal, Uwe (eds.). *Direkte Demokratie*. Berlin, pp. 71-113

Walker, Christopher (2018). What is "Sharp Power"?, *Journal of Democracy* 29(3): 9-23.

Walker, Christopher et al. (2020). The Cutting Edge of Sharp Power, *Journal of Democracy* 31(1): 124-137.

Woodruff, Paul (2005). *First Democracy. The Challenge of an Ancient Idea*. Oxford/New York.

Three Moments in Democracy Promotion Practices of Costa Rica: Towards an Aggregative Process?

Alonso VILLALOBOS-JIMÉNEZ

Introduction

Since the founding of the Second Republic in 1949, Costa Rica has been one of the most stable and complete liberal democracies in Latin America. This democratic stability has not lacked constant struggle among social and political actors for political power, but it has been characterized by a political culture that has promulgated negotiation and gestated temporary social and political arrangements as a way to cope with conflict in diverse situations.[1] Some have also argued that the strengthening of democracy worldwide in the Golden Age of Capitalism was reinforced

---

[0] Opinions expressed are solely my own and do not express the views or opinions of the Costa Rican Ministry of Foreign Affairs and Worship.
[1] Dabene, O. (1999). Democracia y Crisis en América Central: el Caso de Costa Rica. *In* Araucaria 1 (1): 120-132.

internally by social inclusion aimed at improving living and working conditions for most people.[2] For the different territories, this helped expand the range of social and economic opportunities and benefits.

Notably, for more than four decades (1980s-2010s), there has been an academic debate in Costa Rica about a democratic consolidation. The country has made major strides in specifying rights and duties, legitimizing democratic institutions, sustaining the rule of law, and promoting citizen participation.[3] Political representation, however, has been treading water for several decades[4], and the same applies to the deteriorating basic social and economic conditions for democracy – specifically, increased income inequality, stagnating poverty levels, and fluctuating unemployment rates made worse by the COVID pandemic[5]. Also noted is that Costa Ri-

---

[2] Hidalgo, A. L. (2003). Costa Rica en Evolución. San José: Editorial UCR.:16-61.
[3] Furlong, W. L. (2008). Evolución de la democracia costarricense. Partidos políticos y campañas electorales. San José: EUCR.: 255-271.
[4] Rodríguez, F.; Herrero, F. & Chacón, W. (2019). Anatomía de una fractura. Desintegración social y elecciones del 2018 en Costa Rica. San José: FLACSO.: 29-62.
[5] For the recent implications of COVID 19 see: Programa Estado de la Nación. (2022). ¿Cómo está golpeando la

can democracy has given rise to many rights without sustainable public budgets and human resources (public bureaucracy) to ensure respect for those rights, which has engendered increasingly greater support for authoritarian alternatives for solving pressing problems.[6]

In this context of change rooted in the 1980s, Costa Rica opted – sometimes forced by the conditions of its more immediate neighborhood, sometimes by a notion of interested leadership – to develop democracy promotion practices. These promotion practices have been present in most of the administrations since that of Arias Sánchez (1986-1990), especially in the multilateral sphere in both the United Nations system and Central and Latin American integration processes. Since it would be impossible to cover in one article all the details of Costa Rica's foreign policy on this matter, we have chosen to look at three key moments in Costa Rica's democracy promotion practices and later attempt to see if what we are looking at is an ag-

---

pandemia del covid-19 al desarrollo humano sostenible de Costa Rica?. San José: CONARE.

[6] Murillo, A. (2021). Costa Rica: un paraíso verde con los presupuestos en rojo. El País (26 December 2021). https://elpais.com/clima-y-medio-ambiente/2021-12-27/costa-rica-un-paraiso-verde-con-los-presupuestos-en-rojo.html.

gregative process or rather a strong "knee-jerk reaction" to the internal political situation.[7]

Before going into details, we should make a preliminary note of the serious problem of the lack of data, accounting for actions, and record of Costa Rican public spending on democracy promotion. There are some elements to back the statement that democracy promotion is a diplomatic commitment in the country's missions in friendly countries as well as in multilateral United Nations institutions and regional forums.[8] So far, however, we lack accounting and studies on how much the country is investing in this matter. This makes for difficult conversations with friendly countries with a democratic vocation and robust democracy promotion policies, which are even able to indicate how much of their GDP is spent on promoting democracy,

---

[7] This refers to a reflex action. When a doctor taps the patellar tendon in the knee with a small hammer, it causes a spasm in the knee that makes the leg kick forward involuntarily. The analogy in terms of public policy is that of actions or policies being generated in an urgent and imminently situational manner without considering other alternatives that could be strategically and gradually proposed in a planned manner over time.

[8] Murillo, C. (2016). La política exterior de estados pequeños. El caso de Costa Rica. *Temas de Nuestra América Revista de Estudios Latinoamericanos*, 24 (46).

or at least how much of their foreign policy or foreign sector spending is dedicated to this goal. Given the above, the brief analysis offered below lacks economic or financial figures to better illustrate the emphasis placed on democracy promotion by the studied administrations.

Arias Sánchez Administration (1986-1990): Democracy Promotion as a Mechanism to Prevent Conflict Importation

At the end of the seventies, Central America was facing a series of events that would condition the internal political, social, and economic stability of its countries. The conflicts provoked by the oil crises, dissatisfaction caused by the governing elites' unkept promises to extend well-being and economic benefits to more sectors and social groups, and the entrenchment of a repertoire of retaliatory and revolutionary ideologies – used as a basis for organizing paramilitary and guerrilla groups – would lead to a highly volatile political scenario of armed confrontation and political polarization.

In this context, the configuration of international relationships – marked by a new Cold War episode in which the United States was following a strategy of assuring disciplined anti-communist allies – would foster a political culture of win or die.⁹ Added to this, the countries' economic policies were being influenced by the so-called neo-conservative revolution. This revolution impacted most of the Central American countries, which, due to the petrodollar crisis and fiscal and budgetary imbalances were opting for austerity and structural adjustment policies. In the first half of the 80s, these policies would have their own implications in terms of the social situation and income distribution, turning the horizon for collective well-being into a utopian scenario.

El Salvador's civil war, Guatemala's hard-handed anti-insurgent policy, and Nicaragua's revolution (with the respective U.S.-sponsored counterrevolution), in addition to geo-military positioning with U.S. military posts in localized enclaves in Honduras and Panama, shaped an expansive phenomenon of political and social confrontation that for diverse reasons Costa Rica had been able to elude even up to the point when Costa Rican President Monge Álvarez proposed the doctrine of neutrality.¹⁰ During the presiden-

---

[9] Sojo, C. (1988). Centroamérica: Crisis, Potencias y Política Exterior. *Revista de Historia*, n.º 17: 199-204.

[10] Eguizábal, C. (1990). *La nueva estrategia. Administración Monge Álvarez reconstrucción del proceso de toma de decisiones en política exterior (octubre 1984-mayo 1986)*. San

tial and congressional election debates of 1986, however, Costa Rican society began to consider the need for a different focus or approach.

For lack of space, we will not go into detail here on the political and foreign relation factors that led the National Liberation Party's Arias Sánchez administration to involve itself with its Central American neighbors in the pursuit of peace and a cease to armed conflict. We will, however, offer a description of why democracy promotion came into play for this administration as part of its foreign policy.

The central thesis with the most supporting evidence is that in the Central American peace negotiations (with their respective accords, especially in Guatemala, El Salvador, and Nicaragua), the Arias Sánchez administration's foreign policy strategies considered that the accords would be unsustainable over time if they were not accompanied by a set, however basic, of individual guarantees and democratic freedoms.[11] This thesis was partially reproduced not only in President Arias Sánchez's discourse in

---

José, C.R: UCR-IIS.

[11] In this perspective compare: Fernández, G. (1989). El desafío de la paz en Centroamérica. San José: Editorial Costa Rica and Rojas, F. (1992). Política exterior de la administración Arias Sánchez, 1986-1990. Heredia: FLACSO.

his conferences and participations but also in the interventions of his foreign minister, Rodrigo Madrigal Nieto, especially as of 1988. At the same time, elements in the Costa Rican foreign policy discourse underscored the idea that a peaceful neighborhood with democratic stability would be favorable for "attracting business", cooperation[12], and solving other economic issues[13].

We should mention here that a debate exists regarding how this democracy promotion approach employed by Costa Rica had repercussions on the institutional design of Central American integration at the onset of the 1990s – specifically the Central American Integration System (SICA, its acronym in Spanish).[14] The institutional framework in these decades is possibly a kaleidoscope of the interests of Central

---

[12] Sánchez, R. & Ramírez, J.C. (1995). *La cooperación internacional en la coyuntura de la política exterior de la Administración Arias Sánchez 1986/1990*. Heredia: Escuela de Relaciones Internacionales, Universidad Nacional.

[13] Aguilar, M. & Espinoza, A.Y. (1992). La estrategia y estilo de la política exterior: Plan de Paz y renegociación de la deuda externa, administración Arias Sánchez (1986-1990). San José: IIS-UCR.

[14] Rojas, F., & Eguizábal, C. (1989). Política exterior y procesos de decisión en Centroamérica. Elementos para una aproximación a los procesos de negociación regional. *Anuario de Estudios Centroamericanos* Vol. 15, No. 1: 65-80.

American domestic elites. In some areas, such as the environment (materialized in institutions such as CCAD and CAC, for example), an attempt was made to create more democratic or participatory guidelines for actions and interrelations among the states, while in other areas, such as monetary matters and development financing (think SIECA and the BCIE), participatory and democratic values appeared to be superfluous.

What is certain is that the Arias Sánchez administration's foreign policy kept the fire in the neighborhood from spreading to Costa Rican domestic policy.[15] The end of the Cold War and fall of the Berlin Wall was quite convenient for contending with the scale-up and spread of Central American regional conflict.[16] Another contributing factor was the Bush administration's changed approach to Central America.

In October 1989, the Uruguayan president at that time, Julio María Sanguinetti, came out with the phrase *"Where there's a Costa Rican, wherever that may be, there is freedom"*. He did not say, however, that wherever that may be, there would

---

[15] Madrigal, J. (2013). Política exterior de Costa Rica hacia Centroamérica: perspectiva política y económica (1990-2013). *Relaciones Internacionales* 85(1): 143-158.

[16] See again Madrigal (2013) for this matter.

be democracy. Perhaps this is because in the framework of this episode of Latin American history, "freedom" and "democracy" were interlaced, constituting a duality that has endured to the present time. Clearly, questions continue to arise as to whether "long-term freedom" is possible in social scenarios characterized by poverty, social exclusion, and lack of social opportunities for vulnerable populations.

Figueres Olsen Administration (1994-1998): Democracy Promotion for Well-being and a Joint Regional Project

The Earth Summit (UNCED II), held in Río de Janeiro in 1992, led to extensive reflection worldwide on the impact of human activities on the environment and the establishment of international environmental regimes taken on by the United Nations system. Thus was born what was called the "Spirit of Rio", whereby a greater balance of productive activities and environmental protection was deemed attainable under a sustainable development and sustainability approach.

Also in 1992 came the publication of the first global UNDP Human Development Report, which saw development as the *"process of expand-*

ing people's abilities to broaden their choices and opportunities." Both approaches – sustainable development and human development – were to play a discursive role in the Figueres Olsen administration's public policy, particularly its foreign policy.[17] There was already talk in the debates prior to the February 1994 elections of the need for a foreign policy that would focus once again on Central America and strengthen the SICA to promote sustainable development goals.

It is worth noting that President Figueres Olsen (1994-1998), also of *the Partido Liberación Nacional*, took special interest in using foreign policy as a way to dissipate the internal pressures of his administration's first two years, which were peppered with strikes, public demonstrations, and an antagonistic congress – a situation that led him to say that what reigned in the country was ungovernability. President Figueres Olsen also saw that he could exercise significant leadership in the Central American region as a kind of mediator and facilitator in the same manner as the Clinton administration[18]. It should also be

---

[17] Some critics of this approach can be found in: Daremblum, J. (1996). La política exterior de Costa Rica de cara al Siglo XXI. San José: CIAPA.

[18] See the position of his minister of foreign affairs concerning this position: Naranjo, F. (1997). Hacia una política exterior centroamericana. el papel de Costa

pointed out that this administration took special interest in attracting foreign direct investment, for which it argued the need for a climate of social and political stability, not only within Costa Rica but also in the neighboring countries[19].

The Figueres Olsen administration thus promoted among Central American countries an instrument of understanding orchestrated in the light of the Spirit of Rio, which it hoped would also serve as a framework for cooperation and economic policymaking aimed at opening up and consolidating markets. The instrument, called the Alliance for Sustainable Development (ALIDES), was signed in Managua at the end of 1994. The ALIDES stressed that democracy was a pillar of development. More specifically,

... political freedom; respect, protection, and promotion of human rights; combat against violence, corruption, and impunity; and respect for validly signed international treaties are essential elements for the promotion of peace and democracy as basic forms of human coexistence. Peace and democracy are rein-

---

Rica. Capítulos del SELA. No. 50. Caracas: SELA.

[19] Solís, L.G. (1999). La política exterior de Costa Rica en Centroamérica: de la hermandad renuente al activismo fraterno. *In* Paz, integración y desarrollo. Política exterior de Costa Rica 1994-1998. Heredia: Universidad Nacional.: 95-133.

forced through citizen participation. To this respect, stronger democratic institutions, participatory mechanisms, and the rule of law are essential for sustainable development.

From our perspective, Costa Rican foreign policy resumed democracy promotion, arguing that for there to be well-being the rule of law must first be fostered, but later – as the ALIDES states – participatory mechanisms should be encouraged to involve people more in the decisions that affect them. What strikes us is that many of the democratic principles Costa Rica promotes at both the discursive and action levels reflect its intention of driving a third wave of democratization backed by the polyarchy model (the R. Dahl approach), though with some inclination to incorporate social participation in tackling the environmental situation (not so much the social situation) as a contextual element and, occasionally, as an enabling factor for that same democratic transition[20].

During this administration, Foreign Minister Naranjo added the opinion that the good neighborhood was going through not only an absence

---

[20] See: Naranjo, F.E. (1999). Rasgos generales de la Política Exterior de Costa Rica. *In* Paz, integración y desarrollo. Política exterior de Costa Rica 1994-1998. Heredia: Universidad Nacional.: 13-35.

of open political conflict but also the creation of democratic bilateral cooperation arrangements.[21] This was partially reflected in President Clinton's visit to Costa Rica in 1997, when President Figueres Olsen foresaw a fruitful future for both the SICA and Costa Rica's bilateral political and diplomatic relations with each of its Central American neighbors.

The Figueres Olsen administration thus sought to present a joint regional future where democratic institutions would be strengthened along the way, the path to that change was omitted. Likewise, this administration took incipient actions aimed at engendering reflection among SICA authorities on the role that civil society, and especially the Central American business community, should play in this joint project. Strictly speaking, it launched the idea of the need to clarify in what, when, and up to what point social and economic stakeholders should participate and be democratic institution codesigners for both SICA and within the Central American

---

[21] The implications of this position can be seen in two reports: Ugalde, E. (1999). Las relaciones entre Costa Rica y Nicaragua: una delicada e inevitable vecindad (321-354) and Solano, A.E. (1999). Relaciones Costa Rica-Panamá (355-384); both published *In* Paz, integración y desarrollo. Política exterior de Costa Rica 1994-1998. Heredia: UNA.

countries themselves[22]. This reflection was initiated, but it was cut short because the new electoral cycle fostered what has been called "the generation of businessmen presidents", who redefined many of their internal priorities around the Washington Consensus and the deepening of trade relations rather than of political relations.

In general, although it lacked a clear long-term strategy, the Figueres Olsen administration put on the table the idea that democracy promotion should be accompanied by environmental safeguarding and human development promotion. In this administration's view, the enjoyment of democratic freedoms, building of democratic capacities, and primacy of democratic values require a structure, one of robustly and proactively integrated institutions. How to carry this out in practice, however, was not well elucidated.

Additionally, already in the first decade of this century, there was first a distancing and later an ideological and political confrontation between Costa Rica and Nicaragua that imploded with the border dispute between the two countries from 2006 to 2015[23].

---

[22] See for this: Naranjo, F.E. & Solís, L.G. (1999). Una política versátil y creativa. *In* Paz, integración y desarrollo. Política exterior de Costa Rica 1994-1998. Heredia: Universidad Nacional.: 513-518.

[23] Concerning this dispute: Cascante, C., Méndez, M.V.,

Alvarado Quesada Administration (2018-2022): Democracy Promotion as Justification for the Continuation of Democratic Institutions

This administration, the second for the *Partido Acción Ciudadana*, took on two challenges from the start. The first was to carry out a fiscal reform given the pressing rise in public debt levels in terms of GDP, and the second was to drive joint climate change actions in the dimensions of emissions reduction (the project for decarbonization of the economy and establishment of a low-emission public transport system) and climate change adaptation (development of a national adaptation plan as well as regional plans in line with the needs of the different territories).

The first challenge was addressed with a draft law, the result of multiparty negotiation in the Legislative Assembly, aimed at containing spending and setting new taxes. During its negotiation and after its implementation in December 2019, this law would spark significant social discontent, ideological disputes, and recriminations regarding the burden of political and sec-

---

Moya, S., Valverde, J. and Morales, M.F. (2016). Costa Rica y su política exterior 2014: Continuidades y cambios de la administración Chinchilla Miranda a la administración Solís Rivera. San José: PEN-CONARE.

toral responsibility for the debt[24]. Added to the above was a new challenge: The appearance and spread of the COVID-19 pandemic in Costa Rica, starting in March 2020, which led to the closing of the borders, affecting tourism (one of the main sources of foreign currency), and the imposition of public health restrictions, affecting the business activities and freedoms of Costa Ricans.

A recent publication suggests that the Alvarado Quesada government inherited a neoliberal political trajectory that can be categorized as economically regressive, favoring the most powerful economic sectors and turning its back on the country's impoverished and working sectors[25]. Molina and Díaz (2021) point out as well that cuts in the state budget and the new fiscal policy showed the regressive nature of this government's economic vision and its close alliances with the economic elites, which was the real reason for social discontent in 2019. From our perspective, these arguments must be discussed in a broader perspective, including the health and

---

[24] About the internal social confrontations see: Sindy Mora Solano. (2022). Huelga sobre la reforma fiscal en Costa Rica. *Revista de Ciencias Sociales* (174): 13-15.

[25] To this critical perspective see: Molina, I. & Díaz, D. (2021. El gobierno de Carlos Alvarado y la contrarrevolución neoliberal en Costa Rica. San José: Centro de Investigaciones Históricas de América Central, 2021.

social efforts of Alvarado Quesada to deal with the COVID-19 socioeconomic implications. Time will be needed for a more balanced judgement.

These factors are all relevant for understanding, at least from the Costa Rican standpoint, the origins of the proposal for the Alliance for Development in Democracy (ADD). The Alliance was formed in September 2021 during the 76th United Nations General Assembly. At that time, the presidents of Panama, the Dominican Republic, and Costa Rica declared their intention of

... deepening this Alliance as an organization that, through political dialogue, cooperation, and trade, seeks to promote the sustainable, green, resilient, and inclusive development of our countries based on our commitment to the rule of law, democracy, and respect and promotion of human rights and freedom of speech, which we will continue to defend.

We should mention here that the Alliance is based on three operational axes: Political dialogue, cooperation, and an economic-trade axis. In the confluence of these three axes, as of December 2021, the Alliance agreed to undertake an ongoing analysis of the region's pressing problems and solve them through both dialogue and citizen participation and policy consultation, these being understood as pillars of the type of democratic system to which these three countries have historically been committed.

To date (July 2022), there have been three meetings of the presidents in the Alliance and two of the foreign affairs ministers of the participant countries. It is worth noting that in the framework of the Ninth Summit of the Americas in Los Angeles, Ecuadorean President Guillermo Lasso joined this regional group and affirmed the relevance of the platform for Ecuador to share and be nurtured by the democratic commitments and the Alliance while also furthering its participation in the U.S.-ADD Consultative Dialogue on Supply Chains and Economic Growth. We should mention that a working group on supply chains was set up in Los Angeles with a view to creating a joint committee to drive the signatory countries' interest in promoting value chains.

Going back to its origins, in its articles of association, the Alliance agreed to take specific actions on a variety of issues: Regional leadership; migration and refugees; environmental sustainability and climate change; security, justice, and the fight against corruption; and economic growth and work and social opportunities. In all the meetings, however, the presidents have reiterated the urgent need to immediately address the growing irregular migration flows with an integrated approach and the effective co-responsibility of all the countries of origin, transit, and destination in the Americas. These irregular migration flows are seen to pose a threat to internal democracy, since two of the four countries (Costa Rica and Ecuador) lack the financial resources for dealing with them.

The presidents have also been reiterating their concern for the political situation and deteriorating human rights in Nicaragua, especially for the lack of individual guarantees. To this respect, they have urged the Nicaraguan government to release political prisoners and restore all civil and political rights, a request that seems to have fallen on deaf ears in Managua[26]. We should also mention here that although the Alliance has been clear in denouncing the Ortega regime's human rights abuses, it has not come out with a clear statement regarding the foreign policy of nonintervention.

Notably, the Alliance for Development in Democracy has received an accolade from Pres-

---

[26] Nicaraguan policy is currently (2022) exercised by its president and his cabinet and ministers. The current political party in power is the Sandinista National Liberation Front, whose state policy is based – at least discursively – on socialism with a foreign policy of nonintervention in the internal policies of other states.

ident Joe Biden, who described it as a regional example during the closing ceremony of the Summit for Democracy, affirming that it joins together the voices of three countries that are strategic for their democratic political trajectories and historical commitments to the rule of law. The Alliance has also received support from the Canadian and Spanish governments and foresees a bigger commitment from the European Union by the end of 2022. Likewise, a multilateral commitment to encourage and strengthen initiatives that can ensure the sustainable well-being of Central Americans within a democratic framework was reaffirmed in a meeting held in March 2022 between Alliance finance ministers and the CEO of the Central American Bank for Economic Integration (BCIE in Spanish).

In Costa Rica, the minister of foreign relations for the Chaves Robles administration, which took power in May 2022, has affirmed that Costa Rica will continue as an active member of the Alliance. It is still too early to determine, however, if a major shift will be made on this component in Costa Rica's foreign policy and if the Alvarado Quesada administration's level of proactivity will be maintained.

No studies have yet been made on this Alliance or on how much the Alvarado Quesada administration influenced its creation. To this respect, none of the founding presidents has tossed out their authorship. Internally, the Costa Rican media has painted the Alliance as a post-pandemic cooperation platform that has failed to fulfill its initial economic purposes. The issue was notably absent in the electoral debates for the February 2022 elections, except when sporadically mentioned in discussing the relationship Costa Rica should seek with its neighbors to the north.

Our take is that for Costa Rica, the Alliance was an instrument for navigating in times of turbulent democratic coexistence, recurring to a certain legitimacy endowed with reinforced democratic positions and favoring the rule of law shared with two friendly countries. We could argue that Costa Rica has recognized as state policy the universal nature of democratic principles and values in different international instruments, the intention being to ensure democratic institutions and drive dialogue, respect, tolerance, the separation and independence of state powers, and respect for political pluralism and constitutional order as the path to peace and well-being. The Alliance was embedded in this policy with a not only "outward" but also "inward" view.

Our working hypothesis here – which requires empirical evidence – is that in the outward view, the Alliance, from the Costa Rican standpoint, has sought quite specific democracy promotion based on the condemnation of human rights violations in neighboring countries and visibilization of actions against freedom and liberties in Central America as well as the rest of Latin America.[27] Internally, it has sought to provide continuity to the effective exercise of democracy and defend it against multiple internal threats such as authoritarianist proposals, partisan populism, organized crime (especially drug trafficking), and various forms of corruption. We need to verify all this, but we also need to give continuity to how the new administration under Chaves Robles (2022-2026) will orient its foreign policy.

By Way of Conclusion

At the beginning of this article, we asked if the democracy promotion practices implemented in Costa Rica as part of its foreign policy have con-

---

[27] The condemnation of human rights violations is not a novelty; on the contrary, it is rooted in Costa Rica foreign policy. Concerning this, see: Facio, G. (2015). Evolución de la política exterior de Costa Rica. *Relaciones Internacionales* 88, No 2: 19-38.

stituted a habitual process based on prior experience or just "a knee-jerk reaction". Our analysis of the three key moments indicates the first case, though we should not discredit the fact that the implemented democracy promotion practices have been equally influenced by situational factors, especially bilateral relations with neighboring Central American countries.

That said, Costa Rica has not had an explicit international democracy promotion policy that is autonomous from its foreign policy. This has been due not only to budgetary constraints, but also to a consideration of democracy as a primarily internal responsibility (especially prior to the 1980s), even though there are elements suggesting a state policy of commitment to human rights, international law (public and private), and conflict solution through multilateral channels[28]. The foregoing would indicate that for some time both Costa Rican governing elites and political parties have been interested in what was occurring "democratically" in the

---

[28] The continuity of this commitment has been registered by: Zúñiga, F. (2015). Apuntes Sobre la Política Exterior de Costa Rica. Tendencias, Retos y Cursos de Acción, Relaciones internacionales. V. 88, N°1: 11-26. And Lizano, N. (2016). Iniciativas De Costa Rica a Nivel Universal Sobre Derechos Humanos, *Revista Costarricense de Política Exterior*, 26: 25-44.

immediate neighborhood (Central America) and distant neighborhoods (South America and the Caribbean) to the extent that it constituted an internal threat. The three moments analyzed here suggest that this is changing.

On the other hand, although Costa Rica developed degree programs in political science and international relations and installed a diplomatic institute much earlier compared to other countries in the region, the setting up of an academic sub-discipline such as democracy promotion has not evolved naturally. The consolidation of foreign and supranational organizations such as the University for Peace or the Inter-American Court of Human Rights on national soil was needed for turning democracy promotion into an essential chapter for ensuring individual liberties, personal security, and the enjoyment of civil rights. Thus, democracy promotion practices in Costa Rica are based more on its political culture than on programming areas with broad academic and intellectual support. However, we are optimistic that this could change.

To sum up, in its democracy promotion practices, Costa Rica has resorted to forms of implementation that are exemplary of its historical democratic model, which, though not entirely "ideal", is considered the way to solve major social, political, and economic conflicts by recurring to institutions (courts of justice), political negotiation (bargaining and dialogue round tables), and the vote (replacement of those in power through national elections and, to a much lesser extent, the use of the referendum). The abolition of the armed forces can be quoted in this perspective as well[29]. These types of recourses are also backed by the country's positioning in multilateral organizations, as we have noted.

A second recourse has been Costa Rica's promotion of political and trade integration arrangements where democratic principles and practices are respected. Obviously, the Alvarado Quesada administration – unlike the other two moments we have analyzed – looked outside of Central America. The cause was Costa Rican fatigue over SICA, the border conflicts of the Chinchilla Miranda administration with Daniel Ortega's regime, and the substantial cooling of bilateral relations with said regime, which have been reduced to trade relations only[30]. This has also im-

---

[29] This approach as its background in the role of Costa Rican role in the peace negotiations in the 80s can be found in: Rivera, C. (1989). Una Política Exterior de Paz: Costa Rica cree y practica el desarme. Heredia: Escuela de Relaciones Internacionales, UNA.

[30] Public opinion has been playing an important role as

pacted the very identity of democracy promotion practices, which tend to blur when the emphases of the relationship are limited to aspects of trade.

Clearly, what we see as being far off on the horizon is a sort of high-level promotion of democratic practices, that is to say, practices based on other kinds of recourses, such as the development of projects in countries with a democratic deficit, promotion of conflict resolution schemes, programs for helping with internal policy reforms, and assistance and support for organized civil society organizations, among other initiatives proposed by countries with more democratic maturity. The current fiscal and budgetary situation, added to a political culture of urgency and a resurgence of political actors with populist practices in Costa Rica's internal political dynamics, suggests that we will have to wait for another time to achieve such consolidation.

---

well: Pignataro, A., & Cascante, C. (2017). Una sensibilidad focalizada: Opinión pública y política exterior de Costa Rica hacia Nicaragua. *América Latina, Hoy, 77*: 93-114.

About the Author

Dr. rer. pol. Alonso Villalobos-Jiménez is an Associate Instructor in the Department of Political Science at the University of Costa Rica (UCR) and Social Researcher at The Research Center of Sustainable Development (CIEDES-UCR). His work is centered on Costa Rican Environmental Policy, Avoided Deforestation Policies in Central America and Development Patterns in this region. Dr. Villalobos received his doctorate degree in Social Science from the University of Potsdam and a Master Degree in Sustainable Forestry and Land Use Management from the University of Freiburg. He was appointed Ambassador of Costa Rica to the Swiss Confederation in the Alvarado-Quesada administration.

Democracy Diplomacy as Integral Part of Sustainable Development

The SDC's Perspective and Contribution to Democracy Promotion

Patricia DANZI

It is not our diversity which divides us; it is not our ethnicity, or religion or culture that divides us. Since we have achieved our freedom, there can only be one division amongst us: Between those who cherish democracy and those who do not.[1]

Democracy Promotion as Part of Development Cooperation

A recent study of civil society engagement in Tanzania revealed that the public consciousness is occupied far more by immediate everyday

---

[1] Nelson Mandela (2011): Nelson Mandela By Himself: The Authorised Book of Quotations, p. 109.

worries than it is by issues of governance.[2] It comes as little surprise that, in the here and now, clean water, having enough to eat, and sufficient power seem more important than democratic processes, political rights or corruption. Yet this is at odds with the Swiss people's enormous support for efforts to promote democracy abroad and for the government's constitutional remit, which reads: "The Confederation (...) shall in particular assist in the alleviation of poverty and need in the world and promote respect for human rights and democracy (...)".[3]

This inconsistency begs the question of whether promoting democracy should be one of the core businesses of international cooperation, on an equal footing with other Sustainable Development Goals (SDG).

To the SDC, which is used to working in fragile contexts, democratic governance is a crucial means of achieving sustainable development. At the same time, we face the challenge that democracy – or rather democratisation – is often seen as too slow a process to get quick results. More-

---

[2] SDC Tanzania (2022): Assessment of Civil Society and Donor Support in Tanzania, based on Afrobarometer Round 8, Summary of results for Tanzania, 2021.

[3] Federal Constitution of the Swiss Confederation (1999). Title 3, Chapter 2: Powers. Section 1: Relations with Foreign States. Art. 54 Foreign relations. Page 2567.

over, recent developments towards more autocratic governments force us to have a critical look at democratisation.

In my remarks, I will present how the SDC encourages democratisation, why it regards democracy as vital to sustainable development, and how today's challenges impact our work.

Democratic Governance and Sustainable Development

Whether or not development progress is sustainable depends to a large extent on how a country is governed, who holds power, and how that power is exercised and distributed among citizens. It is based on the same principles that underlie Swiss cooperation: Effectiveness and efficiency, transparency and accountability, participation, equality, non-discrimination, and the rule of law. These principles apply at both national and regional levels. The SDC builds on existing local momentum and aligns with universal democratic values rather than promoting specific democratic models:

- Facilitating easy, fair access to information and political participation: This provides citizens with a say in local matters and an incentive to express their opinion. It encourages author-

ities to be more accountable and more transparent.[4]
- Supporting fair, transparent, and inclusive elections helps to create effective, representative parliaments.[5]
- Promoting freedom of the media: Media independence and pluralism are major parts of true and comprehensive information that is available to a broad public and key to holding those in power accountable.
- Furthering decentralised structures: Decisions should be made where their impact is best felt. The key here is effective governance at multiple levels – national, regional, and local. Local governance can act as a kind of "laboratory", to test a democratic system that may not be mature yet at the national level.

---

[4] See: SDC Guidance Sheet: Responding to the Contested Space for Civil Society, Paper based on a Learning Journey in 2018-19.

[5] In the area of election support, the SDC coordinates with the Human Security Division, which works with the Elections and Democracy to Peace (E2P) approach and, in particular, facilitates negotiations on codes of conduct for political parties and candidates to prevent electoral violence. In the area of parliament support, the SDC cooperates with and seeks support from Swiss Parliamentary Services, based on the tripartite memorandum of understanding between the Parliamentary Services, the SDC and the Human Security Division.

- Combating corruption: Corruption hinders basic service provision and is a major obstacle to development in many countries. The embezzlement of public funds also erodes tax revenues and undermines the rule of law. Corruption is a problem not just because it hits the weakest in society hardest, but also because it undermines trust in political institutions and in the political process.[6]
- Supporting inclusive digitalisation[7]: SDC promotes inclusive digitalisation, for example, by using e-governance for better access to services and a more inclusive political process.

Development programmes succeed where enough attention is paid to local political, economic, and social matters. Complex development problems cannot be tackled with technical solutions alone. One needs to understand the institutional and political dynamics of a partner country and its local realities. Therefore, the SDC regards good governance as a crucial lever for all of its objectives.

---

[6] See: SDC Anti-Corruption Guidance.
[7] See: Key Issues in Digitalisation and Governance (SDC Policy Note) and Ways Forward, Assessment Tools and Possible Partners in Digitalisation and Governance (SDC Practice Note).

How to Stay Engaged in the Context of Autocratic Governments?

Democratic backsliding around the globe can also be seen if we track flows of official development assistance (ODA). A recent OECD report revealed that autocratic regimes are consuming an ever-greater share of ODA funding. In 2010, they accounted for 64 percent, but by 2019 the figure had risen to 79 percent. The picture is clear if we look at the relative proportions of populations in these contexts: While 56 percent of people in ODA recipient countries lived under an autocratic regime in 2010, this had grown to 79 percent in only nine years subsequently. For development cooperation actors, working in autocratic contexts has long been the norm. In fact, the OECD classified 25 of the SDC's 35 priority countries as autocratic. Closely associated with this is a greater risk of an abrupt – and often violent – change of regime.

1.1 Staying Engaged: The primary principle of Swiss Development Cooperation

Switzerland's development cooperation work has always revolved around the principle of staying engaged. Autocratic states are no exception here. For one thing, it is important that we engage with the people who are there, who often count or rely on foreign actors to be physically present in countries for their voices to be heard. In addition, we can sustain Swiss investments and existing, well-rooted networks, even if on a smaller scale. By staying engaged, Switzerland can remain a relevant political player and keep channels of dialogue open. The variety of cooperation instruments, humanitarian aid, development and multilateral cooperation offer a toolbox of direct and indirect instruments for promoting democratic values.

1.2 Staying Engaged: What does this entail concretely?

The democratic backsliding that we have witnessed over the past ten to fifteen years hasn't happened overnight. In most cases, the shifts have been incremental, often in the form of constitutional amendments, which appear democratic but, in reality, are rather exclusive. Over the course of its many years of engagement, the SDC has come across many such dilemmas. A set of general parameters for assessing risk and making decisions in politically complex and fragile contexts (see Box 1) guides our work. In addition, the three principles below have proven to be key:

- First, a combination of different foreign policy instruments need to come into play – including development cooperation, humanitarian aid, peace building and diplomacy.
- Second, a broadly diversified group of partners makes a difference. SDC works with partners from the public sector, government, the private sector, the academic community, the media, and many civil society actors. For projects to enjoy long-term success, it is important to have a real partner mix.
- Third, locally driven solutions and country-specific systems are important to strengthen national ownership in the long term.[8]

How can we continue to provide support without giving the impression of endorsing autocratic governments?

Shifting the emphasis of cooperation from a system-centred to a person-centred approach is a way of continuing to support communities. The idea is to re-weight our partnerships towards

---

[8] Working through country systems is enshrined in the effectiveness principle of the OECD. Humanitarian work often operates through parallel structures, since in humanitarian situations country systems may have failed or become dysfunctional. However, efforts are ongoing in humanitarian aid to work more with and through local institutions (localisation of aid).

civil society and other non-state actors as part of a human rights-based approach.[9] Re-weighting does not mean entirely breaking off relations with the authorities. A certain form of cooperation will generally be required to secure access. Maintaining a certain degree of interaction enables us to identify different actors within governments, some more open to dialogue than others. Remaining engaged facilitates jump-starting relations once the environment is again more conducive to systemic cooperation.

How can we promote the process of democratisation in fragile contexts against the odds of autocratisation and polarisation?

Switzerland has a great wealth of experience in promoting democratic development, especially in fragile contexts. Two types of intervention should be mentioned here, one being decentralisation, and the other the understanding of governance as a cross-cutting theme.

- Decentralised, local government has long been a key element of SDC's work to promote democratic governance. Programmes that focus on local-level governance in partnership

---

[9] The human rights-based approach aims equally to empower citizens as rights-holders and capacitating authorities as duty bearers, in a complementary way.

with local communities, civil society and the local authorities improve the way in which local institutions work and increase their accountability. That in turn makes for greater trust between citizens, the authorities and democratic processes. Examples of this type of cooperation include sub-national budget support directed to local authorities as a way of strengthening the system, benefiting basic service provision, and meeting the immediate needs of local communities.
- Governance as a cross-cutting task is to promote good governance through technical approaches and sectoral cooperation. This includes developing and strengthening oversight and accountability mechanisms in the health and education sectors, for example, introducing citizen engagement in reforming water supplies, or improving transparency and accountability requirements with digital and electronic government services.

Although such approaches promote democratic development rather indirectly, they remain vital instruments to encourage democratic values. They don't threaten governments and enjoy a certain success even in heavily polarised and autocratic contexts.

How can we work with civil society actors without creating a parallel society?

The SDC is conscious of the additional strain that is placed on actors in civil society as soon as engagement is transferred from the level of government to civil society.

Long-term sustainable development always requires dialogue with the government.

Alongside a whole-of-government approach, the SDC encourages exchange at the local level. This fosters exchange among local actors. An empowered civil society provides democratic institutions greater legitimacy in the long run. Working particularly with the local media and arts organisations – aiming to keep their spaces open – complements this endeavour. The principle of "do no harm" nonetheless always prevails. Working with our civil society should strengthen it, not put it at risk.

Future of Democratic Governance

All of these approaches support the claim that development cooperation plays an important role in promoting democracy in general and strengthening the Swiss brand of democracy-diplomacy in particular. With its experience in bilateral cooperation, the SDC has a sound understanding of the way in which autocratic systems work. There can be no doubt that the work of the SDC must always be accompanied by a strategic political dialogue with all the relevant actors and through a whole-of-government approach.

Box 1: Risk Parameters for the SDC's Work in Volatile Context

Needs: How have the needs evolved, respectively has the situation deteriorated for the people?

Security risks: What are the security risks to the general population, Swiss staff, local staff and partner organisations and their staff? Can international cooperation programmes continue and, if so, in what form?

Engagement with the government: How much do we rely on cooperation with government actors? At what level – be it local, regional, or national – do we work with the government, and with which sectors, in the sense of political versus technical dialogue?

Financial considerations: Through what mechanisms and partners is the budget channelled, and how is it allocated? Is budget support routed via national, local, sectoral, multilateral or non-state partners?

Reputational risks: What effect would staying in the country, or withdrawing from it, have on Switzerland's reputation?

Principles of engagement: Are there any red lines as far as cooperation is concerned? (Politically, institutionally, or in connection with SDC programmes)?

About the Author

Ambassador Patricia Danzi has been Director-General of the Swiss Agency for Development and Cooperation (SDC) since May 2020. Prior to her engagement with the SDC, she worked for the International Committee of the Red Cross for 23 years in the field, at ICRC headquarters, and lastly as Regional Director for Africa. Patricia Danzi studied in Lincoln, Nebraska, and Zurich and holds a master's degree in agricultural economics, geography and environmental science. She undertook postgraduate work in development studies in Geneva. She speaks seven languages and is the mother of two adult sons.